Chris Dyson Architects   Heritage & Modernity

Chris Dyson Architects

Heritage & Modernity

Dominic Bradbury

First published in 2023 by Lund Humphries

Lund Humphries
Huckletree Shoreditch
Alphabeta Building
18 Finsbury Square
London EC2A 1AH
UK
www.lundhumphries.com

Chris Dyson Architects: Heritage & Modernity © Dominic Bradbury, 2023
All rights reserved

ISBN: 978-1-84822-586-2

A Cataloguing-in-Publication record for this book is available from the British Library

All rights reserved. No part of this publication may be reproduced, stored in a retrieval system or transmitted in any form or by any means, electrical, mechanical or otherwise, without first seeking the permission of the copyright owners and publishers. Every effort has been made to seek permission to reproduce the images in this book. Any omissions are entirely unintentional, and details should be addressed to the publishers.

Dominic Bradbury has asserted his right under the Copyright, Designs and Patent Act, 1988, to be identified as the Author of this Work.

Designed by Tom Green Design
Set in Signifier and Futura
Printed in Belgium

Contents

7	*Foreword: Owen Hopkins*
11	*Introduction*
27	*Residential*
31	Princelet Street, Spitalfields, London
39	Faulkner Residence, Spitalfields, London
47	Gasworks, Gloucestershire
55	The Cooperage, Clerkenwell, London
63	Hampton Lodge, Hurstpierpoint, West Sussex
71	Wapping Pierhead, Wapping, London
79	*Mixed Use*
83	Albion Works, Hackney, London
93	The Queen's Head, Spitalfields, London
99	The Sekforde, Clerkenwell, London
107	Chanarin Residence & Studio, Spitalfields, London
115	Timothy Everest Store, Shoreditch, London
121	Architect's Home & Studio, Preston St Mary, Suffolk
129	*Culture & Community*
135	Maison Colbert, London
145	Eleven Spitalfields Gallery, Spitalfields, London
151	Crystal Palace Park Café, Bromley, London
161	Confer & Karnac, Spitalfields, London
169	*Afterword: Chris Dyson*
174	*Chronology*
176	*Acknowledgements*

Foreword

OWEN HOPKINS

It's still common to see the story of architecture as the story of individual styles emerging one after the other. More fruitful is to think of it as a kind of waveform oscillating over time between different polarities: pluralism and conformity; continuity and rupture; order and chaos; and, looking at the past 100 years, modern and postmodern. Most architects over history sit in one place or another within this; some even move during their careers. But very few evade categorisation entirely. Chris Dyson is one of these few.

Despite building a considerable body of work since establishing Chris Dyson Architects in 2004, Dyson remains hard to categorise as an architect. He is well known for his work with historic buildings, yet the vigour and originality he brings is far from a conventional conservation approach. His interiors have a calmness and even seclusion, yet are also imbued with a profound sense of their urban (or sometimes rural) location. Materials are always carefully considered, both for their inherent qualities and the way they are brought alive through fine craftsmanship. Dyson's is an architecture seemingly without rules, yet at the same time marked by a recurring interest in the interactions between people and city, culture and community.

Dyson has lived and worked in Spitalfields since 1990 and his work is indelibly associated with the area. It's a place that provides a fitting metaphor for his architecture. Over its history, Spitalfields has been subject to waves of new people and cultures, which, rather than sweeping away what lay before, has created somewhere defined by its rich cultural and material layers. It is a place in seemingly perpetual transition, always on the threshold.

Left: Detail of rear elevation of Chanarin Residence & Studio from courtyard garden.

Left: Chris Dyson Architects meeting room at the Queen's Head, 1 Fashion Street.
Right: Cotswold stone meets CorTen at the Gasworks, Lower Slaughter (detail).

And so it is with Dyson's architecture, in which, even with new-build projects, there's an overriding sense of different elements – be they material, temporal or cultural – coming together into coherent wholes. This is, in effect, a process of assimilation, but one that aims not at fusion but at rich and multi-layered syntheses. There are echoes here of postmodern interests in hybridity, and, of course, the time Dyson spent in the office of Stirling and Wilford remains formative. But just as Stirling's later architecture was never straightforwardly postmodern (and his early work never wholly modern), so Dyson's work similarly cuts across both categorisations.

Architecture, for Dyson, is about relationships: to site, to history, to culture, but also to people, whether those in the team at Chris Dyson Architects, the planner, the contractor or the client. These relationships are, by definition, particular to each project, which is why each of Dyson's buildings is different to any other. Yet they are also what connects them, manifested in the way Chris Dyson Architects projects seem like they've always been there, yet are unmistakably also of the present. Dyson's is that rare thing: architecture that feels old and new at the same time.

Introduction

I. HERITAGE & MODERNITY

The houses and buildings designed by architect Chris Dyson carry with them a special sense of belonging. Over the past 20 years, Dyson and his practice have developed a design philosophy characterised by a particular understanding and appreciation of context, which forms a golden thread running through a diverse portfolio of projects. Context, for Chris Dyson Architects, not only means the immediate setting and surroundings of a project, but also the wider neighbourhood, the community and a sense of provenance that encompasses history and architectural heritage. There is clearly a deep-rooted respect for the genius loci and the traces of time that runs through Dyson's work, yet – at the same time – his architecture is decidedly contemporary and clearly belongs to the 21st century.

'We build "new into old" all the time and it has become our USP in a way,' says Dyson. 'Each project is born from a careful analysis of context and place, and this defines the character of our new response. We seek to vitalise contemporary architecture with a rich, inclusive architectural language that fuses the modern movement's ideals of functionality, clarity, integrity and economy with the traditional qualities of form and space, thereby ensuring that our work conveys a sense of historical continuity.'

In many respects, Dyson's approach to heritage and modernity has been informed by his experiences of living and working in the vibrant and multi-layered neighbourhood of Spitalfields. Dyson and his family have made this part of the capital their home for three decades, while his practice's offices are just along the street from Nicholas Hawksmoor's Christ Church, one of the most engaging buildings in East London.

Left: Top-floor staircase in Princelet Street.

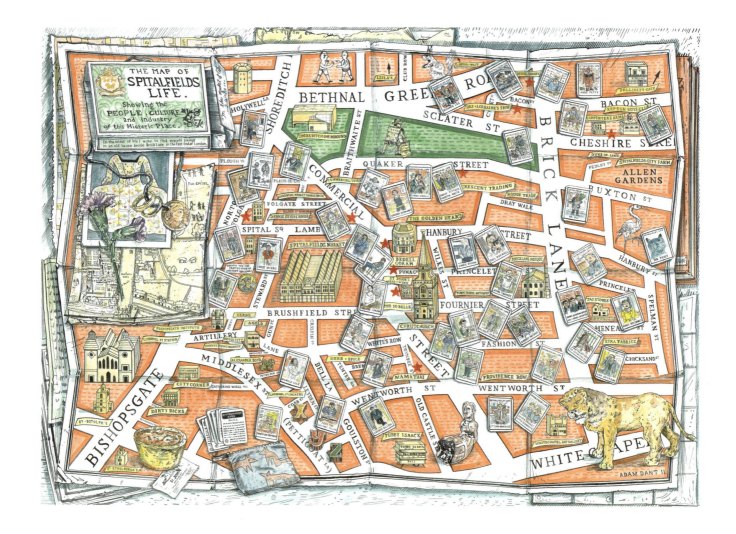

This is, famously, a neighbourhood that brings together a rich mixture of social, cultural and architectural ingredients that are written upon its streetscapes. There are, for example, the elegant Georgian houses that were once home to – among others – the borough's Huguenot weavers and their families. There is a long tradition in the area of silk and wool weaving, textiles and garment making, with small workshops of all kinds proliferating right across Spitalfields and neighbouring Shoreditch. Today, the high-rises and towering financial institutions of the City stand alongside a thriving mixture of retail, hospitality, restaurants and artists' ateliers, as well as apartments and houses, including Dyson's own family home (see p.31) – a restored, remodelled and extended early-18th-century building.

Although Dyson's work now extends far beyond the borders of Spitalfields and Shoreditch, the experience of working in such a diverse and fast-evolving part of London has been both rewarding and informative. Chris Dyson Architects' positive working relationships with heritage advisors, consultants and planners first developed here in East London and the practice's sense of empathy – or the 'sense of shared enthusiasm', as Dyson

Above: Adam Dant's Map of Spitalfields Life.

puts it – has underpinned their work as they have taken on commissions right across London and the country as a whole.

This sense of a strong and clear direction results in projects that might be eclectic in character yet are recognisably Chris Dyson buildings. There is, for example, a commitment to interiors as well as architecture that lends his work an unusual sense of unity and cohesion. Similarly, there is a passion for craftsmanship and artisanal skills, both traditional and contemporary, which overlaps with a love of colour, texture and patina. Above all, there is the sense that Dyson cares very deeply about his work and about where it fits into the wider world. This combination of thoughtfulness and discipline can be traced back to the architect's upbringing and education, and his early professional years working with much respected mentors such as James Stirling, Michael Wilford and Terry Farrell.

II. INFLUENCES & INSPIRATION

There were no architects or designers in Chris Dyson's family to set him on the path to creative practice. If anything, the desire to step into the world of design was a reaction to the traditional professions generally adopted in the Dyson family, with the idea of stepping firmly away from anything that spoke of the 'establishment'.

His father worked for Lloyds Bank, moving from post to post, while his mother worked in medicine yet also pursued an interest in art. Dyson and his sister were born in Yorkshire but his father's work took him to the Midlands, the South East and finally to London. Growing frustrated with the idea of moving from school to school, Dyson asked his parents to enrol him in a boarding school in Leatherhead, where he spent the last five years of his secondary education. Art was one of his favourite subjects.

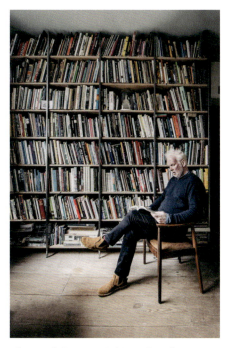

Above: Chris Dyson in his study at home.

'I had a particularly good art master, Mr Clark, who was massively under-employed as there were only a few people studying art by that stage and he was full-time,' says Dyson. 'He encouraged me to at least think about architecture and I thought, "Yes, I will take a look". My father told me it would be a pretty tough profession, as he knew some architects through his work, but he did introduce me to them and I was allowed to go to their offices and follow a few projects. So I went on this voyage of discovery, despite not having an architectural background of any kind.'

Dyson went on to study architecture at Oxford Brookes University, savouring the 'pluralistic' nature of the course and the freedom that it offered to pursue multiple interests. The university gave him a solid grounding in the practicalities of planning and building, yet also the opportunity to explore various threads of architectural history and typologies. One of his university projects, for example, was to design a 'house for a writer', which caught Dyson's imagination; the theme was revisited many years later in the design of a home for Jeanette Winterson (see p.47).

Just as important as the course itself were the friends and contacts made during his university years. These included his wife-to-be, Sarah, who is a linguist and languages teacher, and his future brother-in-law, Harry Whittaker, a conservation architect with whom Dyson has collaborated many times over the years and who now has his own practice in Bath. Another friend from Oxford Brookes and subsequently the Glasgow School of Art is the architect Simon Fraser, who describes Dyson, even as a student, as someone who was constantly picking up inspiration from every possible source.

'He is essentially a magpie,' says Fraser, now a principal at Hopkins Architects. 'He's adept at gathering together seemingly unrelated odds and ends that may seem unremarkable at first glance. However, he can spot the extraordinary and identify something beautiful in the ordinary. This is all part of his design process, whereby these apparently randomly sourced objects inform his building projects and design ideas, sometimes appearing many years later. It is this multi-layered approach which allows him to design so many different types (and scales) of buildings and projects.'

Fraser also recalls how Dyson would be constantly drawing and sketching, even on his travels. During his time at Oxford Brookes, which included a year out in the field with the practice Levitt Bernstein, Dyson managed to save enough money to go travelling in northern India, recording his experiences – including a visit to Chandigarh – in his sketchbooks.

'We visited traditional houses in the hills at Shimla and Ladakh, the lakes of Srinagar and all those places,' says Dyson. 'But it was really wonderful seeing Le Corbusier's work at Chandigarh and the buildings by Maxwell Fry and Jane Drew. I just recall the scale of it more than anything and this vast grid that was designed to be filled but still wasn't at the time, so you could just cut across the grid and these green, empty spaces. I did do a lot of drawing, partly because I couldn't afford to keep buying and developing camera film.'

The habit of sketching and drawing has remained with Dyson ever since, including on family trips and holidays with his wife. In this respect, at least, Dyson is somewhat old-school in embracing the traditional skills of drawing by hand, while also adopting new technology and best practice suited to a 21st-century architectural studio.

Following Oxford Brookes, Dyson and Sarah Whittaker moved to Glasgow, where he continued his studies at the Glasgow School of Art, based in a brutalist teaching block that looked back at Charles Rennie Mackintosh's iconic masterpiece.

'Andy MacMillan was my professor but there were also visiting professors like Isi Metzstein, Doug Clelland, Michael Gould, Paul Keogh and Mark Bains – all these great minds who treated Architecture with a capital "A". It was a very different education to Oxford Brookes, which I would say was more practical, but it was the combination of the two courses that informed my approach to architecture. At Glasgow, I also felt this great affinity with the artist's life, even though I was studying architecture and architects have clients, and those clients have requirements and you need to fulfil those requirements. But there was an affinity and that has influenced things like running my own gallery with Sarah (see p.145), as well as running a practice, and our working relationships with many different artists.'

Dyson was offered the opportunity to continue at the Glasgow School of Art with a master's degree, yet was tempted to London by the offer of a 'dream

Above: Bara Imambara, Lucknow, India.
Above right: Detail of brickwork opening, Ghandi workers' house.

INTRODUCTION

job'. He joined Sir James Stirling's office at a time of growth and expansion, building on a reputation established during the 1960s with landmark projects such as the Engineering Building at the University of Leicester (1963) and his work at both the University of Oxford (the Florey Building at the Queen's College, 1971) and the University of Cambridge (the Faculty of History Building, 1968). Stirling and his practice partner Michael Wilford were looking to expand the office internationally, following commissions for major projects in the US and Germany.

'I just couldn't turn it down', says Dyson, 'and I knew that I had to take the opportunity while it was there. It was still a small practice when I started in late 1989, or early 1990, but they were doing these ambitious competition entries, such as the Bibliothèque nationale de France in Paris and the Tokyo International Forum. Even after James Stirling suddenly passed away in 1992, the office under Michael Wilford was still winning new projects like the Lowry in Salford and the British Embassy in Berlin, so the office was growing.

'And it was just wonderful working with Stirling. It was a very flat structure, rather than hierarchical, so we would have these round-table meetings and

Below: Abando passenger terminal, Bilbao. Sectional perspective by Chris Dyson Associate, James Stirling and Michael Wilford Associates.

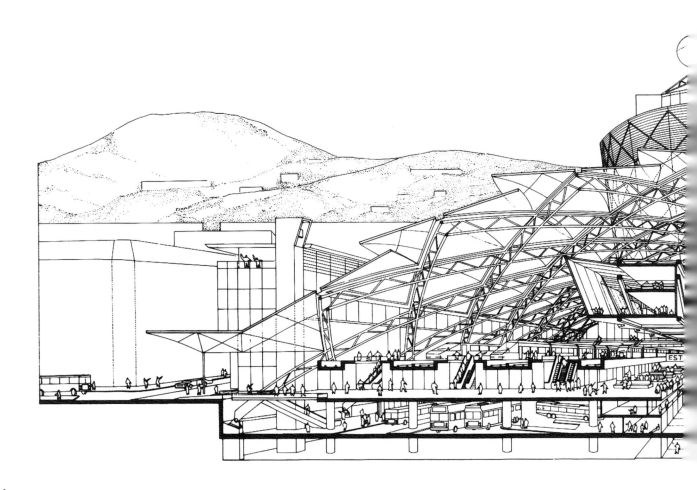

we could talk about our ideas. Jim was like an editor, picking your brains, and then he would run with whatever he thought were the best ideas. He was so open and convivial, and I felt that I got to know him quite well. He would give me special things to work on and I felt trusted, so when he went in for this standard hospital operation that went horribly wrong we were all absolutely shocked. It was a formative time and what we did on every project was invest a lot of time and energy into looking into the history of a place, and then researching and developing ideas that were relevant to that sense of place and how we might abstract them. It was interesting to also look back, as we did, at Stirling's great modern buildings, like Leicester and the Florey Building, and there was more interest in those icons within the group I was working with than postmodern architecture.'

With Stirling's competition entries, in particular, it was as though at least two different styles of architecture were being expressed by the same office at one and the same time, says Dyson. Stirling and Wilford have often defied easy categorisation, but if Dyson took anything from the postmodern strand it would have been a degree of architectural playfulness and warmth, while taking more in the way of discipline, rigour and aesthetic inspiration from the modernist thread of the practice's work.

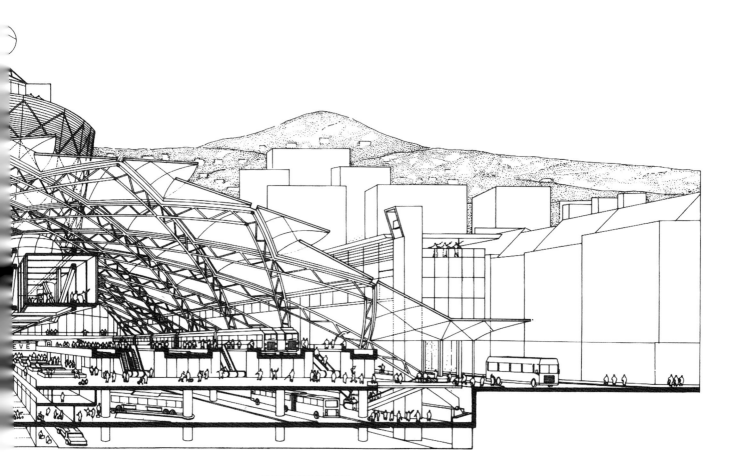

'Stirling was a complete maverick,' says Dyson. 'He was like a sponge, absorbing all these different things. Architects like Stirling absorb ideas, but they still have great integrity in what they do. And he was, ultimately, the author of everything that came out of his office.'

Dyson spent just over a decade working for Stirling and Wilford. He spent a great deal of time in Berlin and Stuttgart especially, running the office's German commissions, with trips back to his wife and family in London at the weekends. There was one Stirling and Wilford project in particular that caught Dyson's imagination, namely a second phase of work at Tate Liverpool during the late 1990s. Stirling initially converted the Victorian warehouse that became Tate Liverpool during the 1980s, but later the practice was asked to return and convert the vacant top floor of the warehouse into additional exhibition and educational spaces.

'I learnt a lot about historic buildings with that project', says Dyson, 'and the idea of heritage as something that should be preserved and enhanced. Because it was both a conservation project and a new build within the framework of an old building, it connected more with what I tend to do now than some other projects.'

Following Michael Wilford's decision to close the practice in the year 2000, Dyson was offered a post as a design director with Sir Terry Farrell's office. As well as projects in the UK, the position with Farrell's practice involved a number of competitions and commissions in China, including the Kingkey Finance Tower in Shenzhen, Guangdong, a 100-storey high-rise that offered Dyson direct experience of working on a highly engineered superstructure.

'It was one of the tallest structures in China at the time,' says Dyson. 'Farrell embraced commercial architecture in an almost American way at that time and was taking on projects that Stirling would never have done. Farrell was also a maverick, but in a very different way to Stirling and Wilford. He was always very supportive, though, and although I was travelling a lot by the end it gave me the confidence to take the decision to set up my own practice.'

By this point, Dyson's own children were growing up and the family was well established in Spitalfields. Then, just as Dyson was thinking about launching his own atelier, Michael Wilford got back in touch about a competition-winning entry for a new Museum of Africa in Stellenbosch, just outside Cape Town. Dyson and Wilford spent nine months working on detailed designs for the museum, with a concept based upon a series of pavilions sheltered under an overarching roof, set within an open landscape of hills and vineyards. Ultimately, the project stalled but it had helped to provide useful impetus to the launch of what soon became Chris Dyson Architects.

Right: The Museum of Africa plan at podium level by Chris Dyson and Michael Wilford.

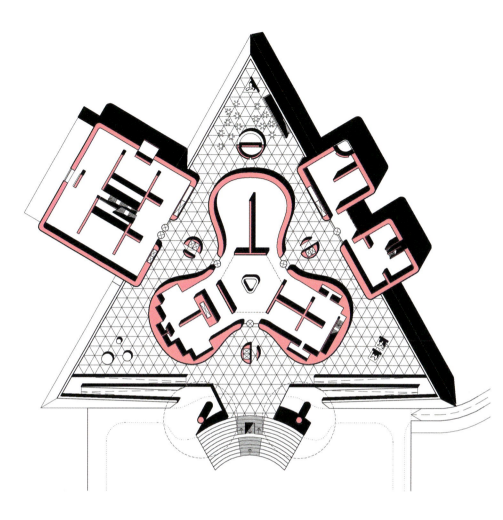

III. WAYS OF WORKING

In many respects, this new beginning offered Chris Dyson an opportunity to break the cycle of constant travelling and refocus his attention upon Spitalfields. Initially, Dyson based his office in a new addition situated behind his family home on Princelet Street (see p.31); later, when the practice expanded, this building was extended and became an art gallery known as Eleven Spitalfields, run by Chris and Sarah Dyson (see p.145).

Many of Chris Dyson Architects' early projects were focused on Spitalfields and Shoreditch, with the principal and his colleagues savouring the opportunity to work in such a unique setting while returning to commissions – like Tate Liverpool – that offered a combination of heritage and modernity, conservation and reinvention.

'Fortunately, Sarah and I, and the children, had been living in Spitalfields for some years by that point,' says Dyson. 'We bought our first house in Fournier Street while I was still working with Stirling and Wilford, and then we moved over to Princelet Street. Coincidentally, James Stirling's ashes are actually buried at Christ Church and he has a memorial stone there; I think he identified with Hawksmoor as a kindred spirit. The fruit and vegetable market was still going when we first arrived and the garment makers were all around us: leathers, furs, jeans, jackets... All these things were being made and sold in Spitalfields. So, we were living cheek by jowl with commercial and residential. When I started the practice, I was able to reconnect with all of that.'

'One of our first projects was formerly a tomato and banana salesman's property on Fournier Street, and the new owners were interested in restoring and extending it. I learnt a lot from that, as well as from working on our own homes, and the tradesmen involved were people that I still have friendships and connections with, and who I still use on projects, today. We have also introduced those artisans to bigger and bigger projects, knowing that they can deliver the quality that we need.'

This artisanal aspect was and is a key element within Dyson's work, including the three homes in Spitalfields that he has designed for his own family and the many residential or live-work commissions within the neighbourhood. The love of collaboration is another constant, with Dyson and his practice making the most of their ongoing relationships with craftspeople of all kinds – joiners, furniture makers, decorative painters and artists – who contribute something valuable to each and every project. Another reference point that crops up many times over in conversation with Dyson is Louis Kahn, but this is not so much to do with Kahn's architecture of monumentality as a shared love of craftsmanship, detailing and texture, as well as materiality. Like Kahn, Dyson truly cares about the patina upon concrete surfaces, and the way that brickwork is expressed, detailed and finished.

Authenticity is a constant concern, with the practice committed to architecture and interiors of quality and integrity. Clearly, this is an understandable preoccupation when it comes to listed and period buildings, yet it also carries over to the way in which old meets new, with clear boundaries and dividing lines between – for example – an 18th-century building and its new, contemporary extension. For this reason, blurred lines and pastiche are anathema.

All of these elements are rooted in research. The practice's projects begin with a detailed research process that looks to establish the historical, social and cultural context, as well as limitations and possibilities related to planning and precedent. This applies not only to the many listed buildings that Chris Dyson Architects has been involved with, but to every project. Dyson offers the example of the Confer & Karnac bookshop and cultural space in Spitalfields (see p.161). Here, the context was actually a former

Above: Charcoal drawing of Christ Church, Spitalfields, for Article 25.

Above: Puma Court in the 1970s showing post-war bomb damage.
Above right: Folgate Street finished build, 2023.

factory dating back to the 1930s, which once made sequins for the local garment trade. As revealed by the initial research process, the original building was semi-industrial in character, which generated a design proposal that was not only tailored to meet a very specific brief from the clients but also to respond to the history and provenance of the building itself. The choices of materials, fenestration, finishes and colours were all informed by research and context.

'We love the historical research phase and it often runs simultaneously with getting a set of survey drawings done,' says Dyson. 'Usually, we find that no measured drawings are available so we will send a surveyor over to get them drawn up, so we know exactly what we are working with. At the same time, we will be doing some enthusiastic research about the locality and the history of the building or the site. We might also have a heritage consultant who would prepare a report for us, but also reveal their findings on a more periodic basis as they progress.'

'For more complex sites, we might have a morphological plan that shows us how buildings and their footprints have changed over time, including what has disappeared and what remains. That becomes an important part of the

INTRODUCTION

heritage story and, if you can illustrate how a building has evolved, that can affect what happens to it in the future. It shows that we have understood and recorded the evolution of the site, and suggests how we are going to respond with a new project that will be the next step in this evolution.'

Archival research and morphological plans often uncover surprises, secrets and ghost buildings. A site or streetscape might reveal itself to be a kind of architectural palimpsest, which has been reused and repurposed many times over, and this needs to be understood not only for poetic or artistic reasons related to a contextual design solution, but also in terms of constructing a convincing argument for change that will persuade the local planners and conservation officers.

'This word "palimpsest" is very interesting to us,' Dyson says. 'Like an ancient parchment or manuscript, you start to see this layering of a house or a street at different times. It is like finding ghosts and they manifest themselves in different ways, like street names or signage, for example. When you start to peel back the layers of paint on a building, you might find a shop sign or the original paint colours, which can help inform the design process.'

Equally, with new-build projects the research phase to establish the wider context of the project and the provenance of the setting can be vital. Such was the case,

Below: Crystal Palace Park Café.

Below: The dinosaurs by Benjamin Waterhouse Hawkin in Crystal Palace Park.
Below right: Conceptual collage by Chris Dyson for cladding of café, connecting the history of the site with our new building.

for instance, with Chris Dyson Architects' new café for Crystal Palace Park (see p.151), which which is located within the parkland laid out by Joseph Paxton around the site of his majestic Crystal Palace. Although the palace was lost to fire during the late 1930s, many traces of Paxton's listed and protected pleasure garden still remain. All had to be fully appreciated, respected and understood before the design process could even begin.

'The Crystal Palace Park Café was one of our first public projects, as an amenity space for the community,' says Dyson. 'It was a new building designed to replace a 1950s café that had seen better days but it sits within this historic context of the palace, the landscape and the listed dinosaur sculptures by Benjamin Waterhouse Hawkins. So there were all these back stories and elements that we needed to explore. Eventually we decided to coat our new building in cedar shingles with a rounded edge that have a deliberate but subtle sense of connection with the dinosaur scales seen in the sculptures in the park.'

Such references are often very subtle, forming part of a project designed to meet a working brief, yet these details help to create that special sense of belonging. Without the shingles and scales, as well as other contextual references, the café would still be an elegant building but one that could exist almost anywhere. It is this notion of a building that belongs to its genius loci that helps to set Dyson's work apart.

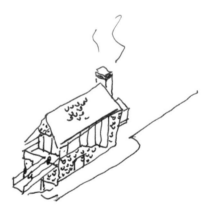

INTRODUCTION

'We were really pleased with the café because we combined the idea of doing an original, brand-new building but within a listed parkland setting,' says Dyson. 'Similarly, with the Harrow Arts Centre, we are working on a brand-new building but in a heritage setting surrounded by listed buildings. There's something really rewarding about these kind of projects because they involve local people and the community in a very direct way. Private commissions are lovely, and remain the mainstay of the practice, and I would never undermine that. But with public projects it's a very different thing and you are affecting the lives of many different people, hopefully for the better.'

IV. PAST & PRESENT

All of Chris Dyson's projects – whether new-builds or the conversions and reinventions of period buildings – involve this constant creative dialogue between the past and the present. The projects that follow begin with a chapter on residential work, which, as Dyson says, has formed the foundation of the practice for many years. The second section is devoted to mixed-use projects, which reflect Chris Dyson Architects' continued interest in diversity and multifaceted streetscapes and neighbourhoods, where all kinds of activities and pursuits result in a continual process of cross-fertilisation and renewal. The third and final section, including the Crystal Palace Park Café, is devoted to cultural and community projects, with a particular emphasis on commissions that overlap with Dyson's own sense of commitment to the world of art.

This book includes projects of very different kinds and in very different settings. And yet, for the reasons outlined above, Chris Dyson Architects' portfolio to date is remarkably cohesive, reflecting an ongoing allegiance to contextuality, craft, culture and community. Undoubtedly, the practice will continue to work in fresh settings and situations, with a number of important new commissions already underway in England, Scotland and Italy. Yet there's also little doubt that Chris Dyson's buildings will always reflect their surroundings and will always feel as though they belong.

Right: Portrack House extension, drawing by Elia Loupasaki.

Residential

From the launch of his practice back in 2004 through to today, residential work has formed a key part of Chris Dyson's portfolio. Many of these projects, including Dyson's own family home (see p.31), have been focused on Spitalfields, where Chris Dyson Architects also has its offices. Set within the unique context of such a characterful neighbourhood, where period buildings rub up against the modern towers of the City, Dyson's Spitalfields commissions convey – as he puts it – a 'sense of historical continuity'. 'We are striving for synthesis between traditional buildings and the current requirements for more fluid and flexible design,' says Dyson. 'But, above all, we hope to maintain the connection between suitability of purpose and beauty.'

Dyson's family home on Princelet Street manages to neatly encapsulate this design philosophy. In many ways, this was a restoration project that sought to reinstate the 18th-century facade and the character of the building as it looks out on to the street. Yet Dyson also took the opportunity to add a fresh storey at the top of the building that now holds the kitchen, dining area and a roof terrace within a decidedly modern solution to the challenge of creating welcoming, sociable and enjoyable family-centric spaces. The Princelet Street project also offered the chance to create a flexible space to the rear of the property that served initially as the practice's own offices and then as an art gallery (see p.145).

Left: Top-floor kitchen and dining room at Dyson's home, Princelet Street.

Increasingly, Dyson's commissions have taken him far beyond Spitalfields and its neighbouring communities, with projects out in the counties, Scotland and abroad, including Italy. Yet many of the practice's rural commissions have also involved the delicate interplay between tradition and modernity, as well as between conservation and reinvention. The Gasworks commission in Gloucestershire (see p.47), for example, saw Dyson radically extending a period stone cottage by picking up on the unusual history of the site, which had once included a gasholder that helped to provide a source of lighting for the grand country house nearby. This long-lost cylinder and other outbuildings provided a key source of inspiration, but also a precedent for the thoughtful 21st-century addition that ultimately transformed the property.

Above: Study tower and circulation, Gasworks.
Right: Internal view of our proposed roof extension to a property on Tenter Ground, drawing by Elia Loupasaki.

Other interventions have been more modest and subtle, yet also transformative. With Hampton Lodge (see p.63), in West Sussex, much of the project was about restoring and gently updating a listed mansion dating back to the 1830s. Yet, at the same time, Dyson and his clients decided to refocus the interior layout for modern family living by transforming a large reception room into a spacious kitchen and dining area that is now right at the heart of the house and family life.

Both projects, and the others that follow across the coming pages, also provide prime examples of the importance of the creative dialogue between architect and client. Such collaborations have clearly been uplifting for Dyson himself, and for his practice, especially when it comes to the highly individual challenge of creating rooms and retreats that reflect the needs and personalities of those who will ultimately call such spaces home. 'Behind every successful building is an engaged and proactive client,' says Dyson, 'who makes a unique contribution to the development of the brief and the evolution of the design.'

Princelet Street, Spitalfields, London

Sitting on the edge of the City but with a unique history and a character of its own, Spitalfields has been a key focal point for Chris Dyson and his family for three decades. Dyson and his wife Sarah, a teacher of modern languages, first settled here during the early 1990s when they restored a house on Fournier Street, just across the road from Nicholas Hawksmoor's Christ Church. Not long after this, they spotted an empty house on nearby Princelet Street and wrote a friendly letter of enquiry asking if the house might be for sale. The answer took ten years to arrive, during which time squatters moved into the house, but eventually they heard that the house was being sold and the Dysons submitted a sealed bid. Soon, Dyson found himself working on another personal project, which involved an all-encompassing restoration and reinvention of the terraced building.

'The original house was built in the 1720s and was owned by a French Huguenot clergyman, so the bones of the structure date from that period,' says Dyson. 'But the front elevation had been altered because it was used by a company called Jackson & Joseph as a factory making workwear from the 1930s onwards and then as a Bengali cooking school. The original windows had gone and there were these horizontal slots on the first and second floors. So it looked as though the facade needed mending and the house seemed like this broken tooth in the street.'

The only surviving 18th-century ingredient was the staircase, which was retained and restored, but the rest of the house required rebuilding as well as modernisation to create a contemporary family home for the Dysons and their two children, Oliver and Bella. The factory-like facade was taken down and rebuilt in a manner fully sympathetic to the neighbouring buildings, including Georgian windows with red-brick surrounds and keystone arches above, as well as a shop-front style treatment for the ground floor complete with window shutters. But behind the facade Dyson reworked almost every part of the house apart from the existing panelled staircase.

Left: Dyson's home, and former studio and gallery.

'We took a fresh take on the house,' says Dyson. 'With the spaces that we felt we really had to restore, like the sitting room, we wanted to make them look and feel original. So we built the timber panelling in the sitting room, for instance, very much as it would have looked in the 18th century. But when it came to completely new spaces, like the kitchen and dining room on the top floor, we designed those as very contemporary rooms with no apology for that.'

The result is a fusion of past and present, but one united by a sense of cohesion and order over all five storeys of the building. This is helped by a carefully curated palette of warm, natural materials and soothing colours that help to tie the interiors together, while services and modern technology are hidden away behind the panelling and tucked into the structural fabric of the building.

On the ground floor, Dyson created two elegant, interconnecting rooms that can serve variously as a library, a meeting room or an event or exhibition space. Beyond this, in what was once the clergyman's courtyard garden back in the 1720s, a former joinery workshop has been fully reinvented to provide a top-lit space, where the Dysons ran an art gallery (see p.145). The entrance hallway also leads through to the staircase that carries upwards to the family's private realm, with the panelled sitting room at first-floor level overlooking Princelet Street, plus one bedroom to the rear, while two further family bedrooms and a bathroom are situated on the second floor.

Above left: First-floor sitting room.
Above: Staircase gallery.

Ground floor

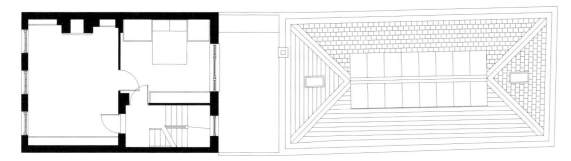

First floor

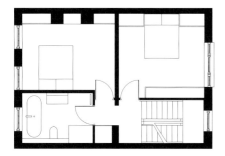

Second floor

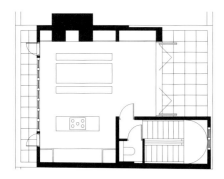

Third floor

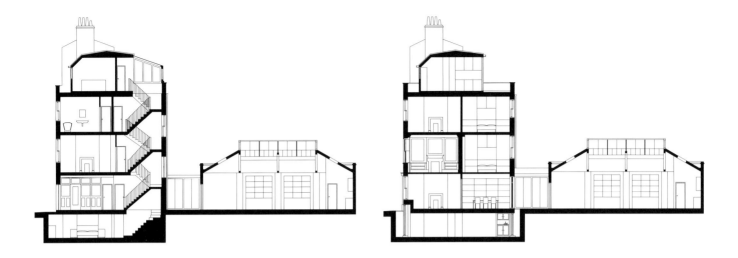

Above: Section through staircase.
Above right: Section through accommodation and studio.

Dyson secured planning permission for an additional level at the top of the house, holding the kitchen and dining room, as well as a modestly scaled roof terrace. In the neighbouring houses, this mansard level would have been occupied by the weavers' lofts common to the neighbourhood, but – given the history of this particular house – a loft was never added, creating an opportunity to even up the roofline of the terrace with this welcoming new floor, lifted by the quality of the light and the views out across Spitalfields.

'It gives us a private family space where we can come together in a rather unconventional but comfortable fashion,' says Dyson. 'As a family, we do spend a lot of time in the kitchen and ours is a real contrast to many other Spitalfields houses, where the kitchen is down in the basement. You suddenly have one of the best spaces in the house being used all of the time.'

The basement level, meanwhile, has been converted into a self-contained studio, adding to the way in which the remodelled house provides a range of spaces within the same building and is suited to a variety of purposes. While the Princelet Street house remains a much-loved family home for the architect and his family, the mixed-use model has helped to influence other projects where many different things might be happening under one roof (see Mixed Use, pp 79–128).

'I learnt a lot from the process of working on this house,' says Dyson. 'The colours have to work and flow from room to room and the experience needs to be calm, without too many violent changes between the spaces. But also, it is a good example of live-work and there are now a lot of these kinds of buildings in Spitalfields and it's helped to bring back some of the original vibrancy of the neighbourhood. The character of Spitalfields is shifting but it has changed for the good in many ways.'

Left, clockwise from top left: Staircase; first floor drawing room; first floor landing; family bathroom.

RESIDENTIAL: PRINCELET STREET

Above: Drawing room.
Left: Stairs to kitchen.
Right above: Terrace and south windows.
Right: Dyson sketching in kitchen.

Faulkner Residence, Spitalfields, London

Strikingly grand for Spitalfields in terms of its stature and scale, the Faulkner Residence is a former merchant's house that sits between Commercial Road and Bishopsgate. With five storeys and five bays, the house is an elegant presence on White's Row, sitting almost opposite to the former Fruit & Wool Exchange. Here, Chris Dyson was asked to create a spacious family home while restoring the historic fabric of the 18th-century building, which had been neglected for many years.

'It does look very grand, with this central entrance hallway and staircase with rooms to either side,' says Dyson. 'The frontage to White's Row had been painted lemon yellow so we removed all of the paint and restored the brickwork and pointing, as well as putting back the arched timber sash windows. All of these original details have been restored and there is a stepped staircase up from the street to the front door, with a lower ground floor below, which adds to the character of the house.'

The two key challenges faced by Dyson and his clients, a Magnum photographer and a City investor, were how to create a home better suited to contemporary family living and provide green space within a building that was tightly landlocked. As with the Cooperage (see p.55), the decision to excavate downwards to open up additional living space at basement level was transformative, especially in combination with a top-lit conservatory to the rear of the building, which has been slotted into a narrow space once occupied by a courtyard.

Left: Top-lit dining room.

'A house like this would have had a garden at one time but obviously that had been sold off over the years and had been lost, so all that was left was this small courtyard, which was open to the sky when we started work on the project,' Dyson says. 'So we colonised the courtyard by enclosing it with glass and making it double-height, while making an internal, vertical garden, which continues upwards on the boundary walls above and beyond the conservatory.'

The new conservatory manages to serve many key functions within a single space. It is a welcoming garden room but also a light well, which draws sunlight all the way down to lower ground level, as well as helping to illuminate the rear windows of the house that look over the conservatory. But it is also a key family living space, providing a generous dining area that connects with the kitchen alongside it, while the toplight and the crisp, white side walls also make it well suited to displaying artwork.

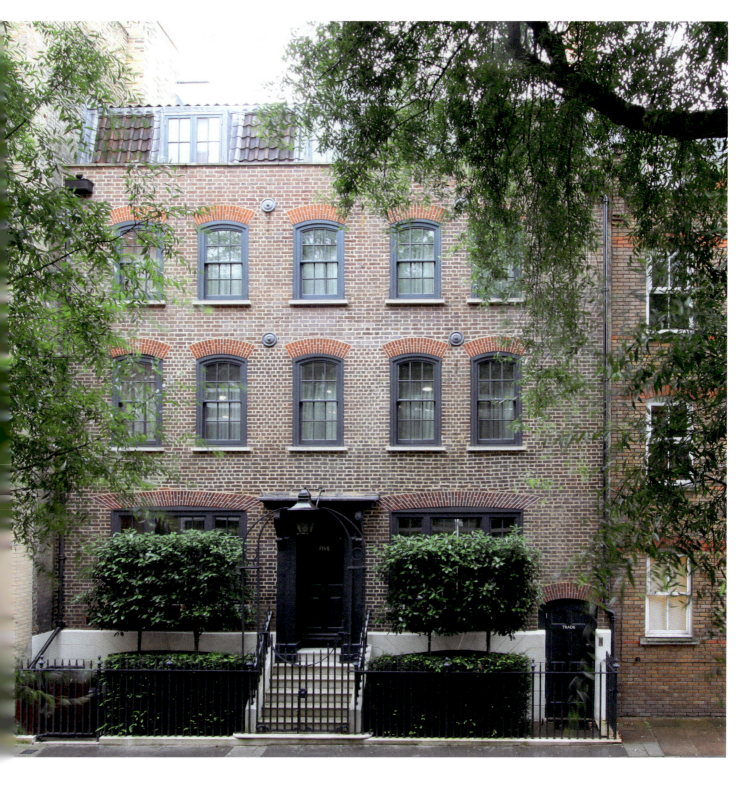

Left above: Sketch of White's Row context.
Above: The restored facade.

'The house is spacious, as it needed to accommodate a large family with children, so it is very much a family-sized home with all the spaces that they would need,' says Dyson. 'Having filled in the courtyard we also decided to add a roof terrace at the top of the house, where we rebuilt the mansard because there was a lot of structural rot and damage.'

The third-floor mansard level now holds a master suite, with four further bedrooms on the first and second floors. The reception rooms on the raised ground floor either side of the staircase were expertly restored, with period elements and original features preserved as far as possible, yet modern comforts, such as underfloor heating, were introduced throughout. The timber-panelled spaces, in particular, provided opportunities for introducing colour and texture, with the soft greys of the sitting room, for example, giving way to the vivid arsenic green of the adjoining study which looks over the conservatory and the vertical walls of planting.

The Faulkner Residence, which sits within the boundary of the former Tenter Ground Estate and was once part of a streetscape lined with Georgian houses, offers a vivid example of the careful architectural balancing act that ensures both restoration and revival. The original detailing and craftsmanship have been fully respected, yet welcoming and contemporary spaces have also brought a fresh dimension to this historic period house.

Right: Cross section of the house.

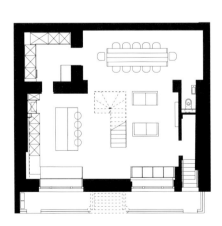

Lower ground floor

Ground floor

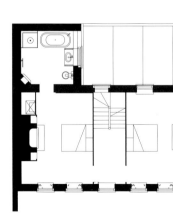

First floor

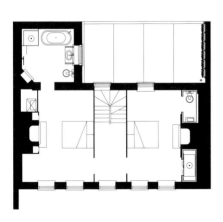
Second floor

Third floor

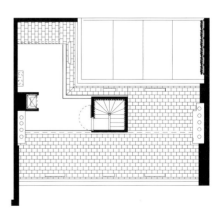
Roof terrace

RESIDENTIAL: FAULKNER RESIDENCE

Above left: Study window.
Above right: Stair landing view.
Left: Green wall.
Right: Dining room and kitchen study window.

Gasworks, Gloucestershire

As an architectural student at the Glasgow School of Art, Chris Dyson worked on a conceptual idea for a writer's retreat. It was an unusual and escapist project that Dyson recalls with great affection, especially as he was eventually able to explore the idea further with a countryside sanctuary designed for the novelist Jeanette Winterson.

The architect and writer already knew one another before the project began, having met in Spitalfields, where Dyson had advised Winterson on updates to her Georgian listed home. The context of the Cotswolds was very different, of course, yet also involved a listed building and what the writer has described as a 'new/old solution'. Winterson had purchased a small stone and slate cottage, which sat alongside the remnants of a gasworks that supplied the source of illumination for a Victorian country house nearby. Little remained of the gasworks itself beyond a footprint and history, yet the local conservation officer suggested that the simplest way to gain planning approval to extend the cottage as Winterson wished would be to reuse the footprint of the ghost buildings.

'Enter Chris Dyson, a Spitalfields architect who is inspired when it comes to finding a language between old and new structures,' Winterson said of the project, which makes use of Cor-Ten steel for the new additions. 'A new rusty steel barn defines the envelope of the building, acting as a holistic "wrap" which gives homage to the old industrial character and form but at the same time a modern, sustainable annexe which makes a delightful contrast to the main building.'

Left: The new Cor-Ten annexe.

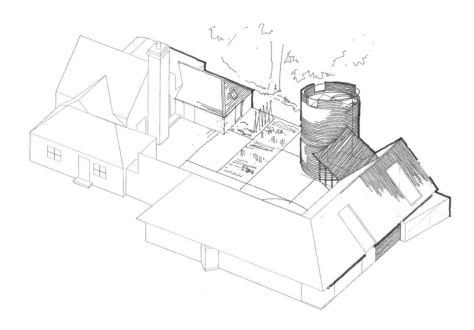

Left: Axiometric view of the project.
Right: Roof plan of site layout.
Below right: Ground-floor plan.

Dyson proposed devoting much of the original stone cottage to the living spaces, including a kitchen, dining area and lounge. A slim, glass-sided link leads from the cottage to a largely single-storey and U-shaped addition, which follows the line of the lost buildings while helping to define and protect a central courtyard space. A circulation corridor carries past a set of new bedrooms and bathrooms, which look out across the gardens, until it eventually reaches a two-storey, silo-shaped cylinder, recalling the shape of the old gas storage tank but now holding writing and study spaces at both ground- and first-floor level; the latter, in particular, offers open views out across the surrounding landscape.

'It looks like a complex or collection of buildings in an almost Japanese style, rather like pavilions,' says Dyson. 'And, given the gasworks' history, we decided to clad the annexe in Cor-Ten steel. The beautiful thing about Cor-Ten is that it starts to weather so quickly and seems to harmonise so well with other more natural materials, whether it's red brick or Cotswold stone. It falls into the tradition of a low-cost, industrially made material but with this beautiful aesthetic quality.'

Cor-Ten purposefully forms a protective coat of exterior rust, which has an earthy, almost organic quality, making it well suited to rural as well as urban settings. Here, the steel plates give the cylindrical study tower a highly sculptural quality, but also help to unify the annexe as it wraps its way around the garden court, while the carefully considered pattern of fenestration frames key views.

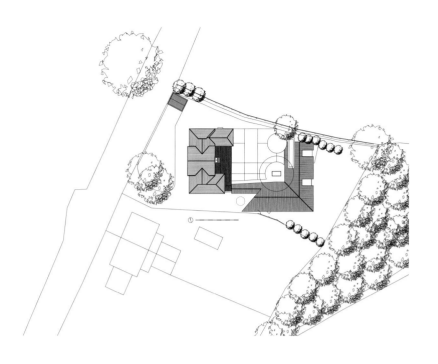

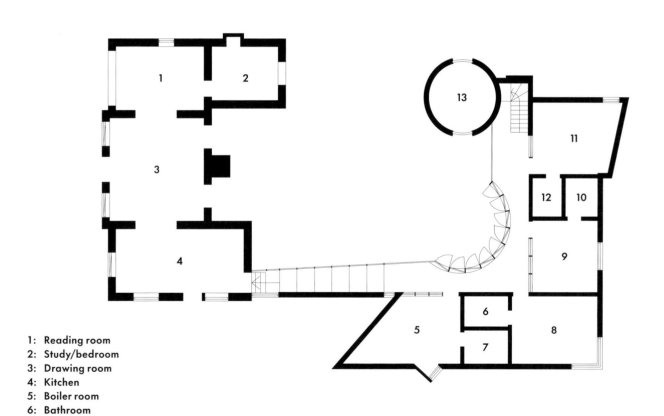

1: Reading room
2: Study/bedroom
3: Drawing room
4: Kitchen
5: Boiler room
6: Bathroom
7: Bathroom
8: Bedroom
9: Bedroom
10: Bedroom
11: Bedroom
12: Bedroom
13: Writer's tower (two circular study rooms)

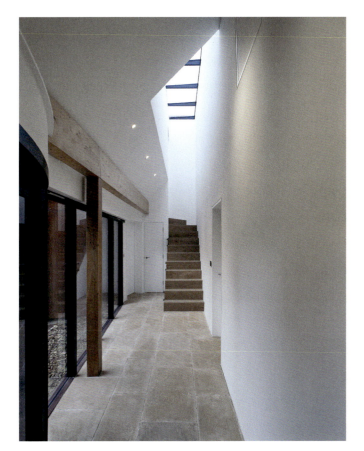 

Left: Study tower.
Above left: Corridor cloister.
Above right: Cotswold stone meets Cor-Ten steel.

After planning permission had been obtained, Winterson's circumstances then changed and the project was passed on to two other writers, who embraced the plans and carried them forward. Like Winterson, Dyson's new clients wanted to ensure the building's green credentials, with a structural timber framework combined with high levels of insulation. A combination of an air source heat pump and a wood pellet boiler provides heating and hot water.

'The new clients were also very keen on the house being as sustainable as possible, with a low carbon footprint,' says Dyson. 'And the Cor-Ten cladding involves minimal maintenance, with no repainting and a coat that just gets better with age.'

There are also echoes of the vernacular here, with something of a barn-like quality to the annexe, as Winterson has suggested, as well as a sculptural element. But importantly the new addition respects the original cottage alongside, without trying to overwhelm it. And, certainly, there is a strongly escapist character to the completed house, as befits a writer's sanctuary.

The Cooperage, Clerkenwell, London

Working within the context of densely layered, historic neighbourhoods such as Clerkenwell inevitably offers multiple challenges when it comes to creating a fresh family home, as well as many rewards. The Cooperage provides a dramatic example, with this former Victorian barrel-making warehouse tucked away in the backlands of the streetscape and accessible only through a narrow alleyway while being surrounded by neighbouring buildings on all sides. Here Chris Dyson and his practice managed to design what could be described as an engaging urban retreat, which provides a welcoming and restful sanctuary, especially during the evenings when the surrounding offices are quiet.

'It's a secret house, in a way, because nobody really knows that it's there, even though there are 6500 square feet [604 square metres] of living space,' says Dyson. 'You can be quite anonymous living in the house but still enjoy the luxury of space and the quality of the build. You are in this courtyard in the heart of Clerkenwell, which is busy and bustling during the day, but relaxing here in the evening is lovely, enjoying the roof terraces that we created, which was one of the key elements of the project.'

The substantial brick building, which sits within the Clerkenwell Green Conservation Area, was first converted to residential use during the 1990s. But, having acquired the warehouse, Dyson's clients wanted to take a much more ambitious approach, creating additional living space both indoors and out while also opening up the existing building to create dramatic family spaces with a striking sense of openness, height and volume.

The practice's plans involved digging out a new basement level but also extending upwards to create additional bedrooms and terraces. With over 25 party wall agreements to be sorted out with neighbouring properties it was, perhaps, to be expected that there were some initial objections to the proposals. But Dyson's ideas were actively supported by the local conservation officer, who had noted an elegant model of the project presented at the Royal Academy of Arts Summer Exhibition, including the sculptural addition at the top of the warehouse, clad in characterful brass panels.

Left: Triple-height drawing room.

'We chose brass for the new addition at the top because we wanted something that would contrast with the original brick,' says Dyson. 'It is this unashamedly modern element above what is essentially a Victorian cooperage, but the conservation officer at Islington Borough Council supported us through thick and thin. The two roof terraces are on different levels, with one of them benefitting from the west light in the evenings and then another right on top of the main body of the house, which gets the sun all day long and has nothing overshadowing it.'

The interiors were transformed by the decision to dig out the new basement. The main entrance remains at ground level, of course, but the entrance hallway is now essentially a mezzanine floating above the main living spaces on the sunken floor below. Here, the living room and dining room are now soaring double- or triple-height spaces, while the kitchen alongside is lightly defined by its position underneath the mezzanine. While the seating zone features a dramatic wall of raw, red brickwork anchoring a floating fireplace and flue, the dining area is top-lit by a retractable skylight that draws light over the green, planted wall to one side. Concrete floors with underfloor heating help unify these open and fluid living zones, while the new staircase that sits at the heart of the plan serves as a key focal point.

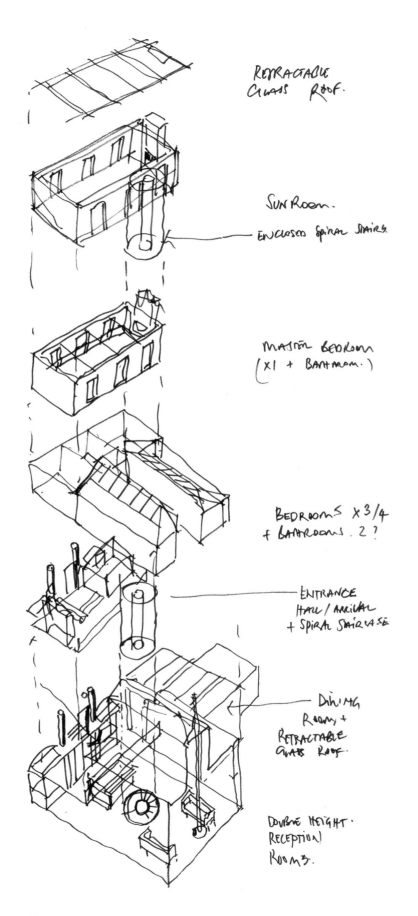

Left above: Elevation in context.
Right: Exploded axiometric of early sketch proposals.

RESIDENTIAL: THE COOPERAGE

Left: Living, dining and kitchen areas.

'The suspended, free-standing steel and timber staircase rationalised the vertical circulation and pays homage to the building's industrial past,' says Dyson. 'One of the most pleasing aspects of the project was the level of aspiration in terms of quality along with the specialist design elements, such as the new staircase and the roof light over the dining area.'

There is a vibrant juxtaposition throughout the interiors between the suitably industrial finishes, which connect with the building's past, and warmer materials such as the French oak floors for the bedrooms. Integrated storage and fitted furniture in many different parts of the house allow the spaces themselves to remain relatively uncluttered, enhancing the overall sense of space.

'There was a very patient builder who knew how to achieve really good finishes, so it was a pleasure to work with him,' says Dyson, of the RIBA-award-winning project. 'But the clients also had real tenacity and were used to dealing with intellectually demanding situations in their day jobs. To their credit, they did a wonderful job and made a lovely house for themselves.'

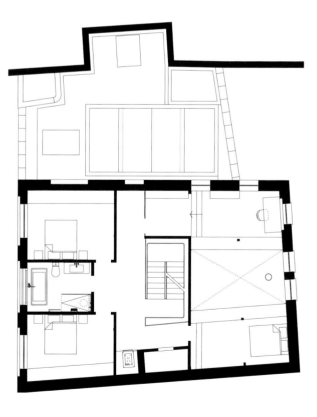

Basement

First floor

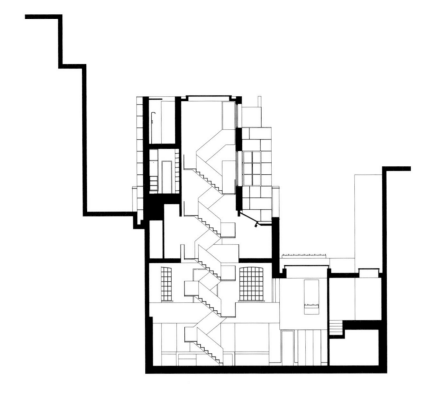

Above: Cross section East–West.
Below: Cross section North–South.
Right: Front door onto the yard,
new brass-clad extension above.

Hampton Lodge, Hurstpierpoint, West Sussex

Many of Chris Dyson Architects' recent residential projects have required a careful balancing act, involving respecting the period provenance of a house while updating it for modern living. This is true of homes in both town and country, including this substantial Grade II listed property in West Sussex dating from the 1830s. Back in 1837, a local history of the village of Hurstpierpoint, which is situated to the north of Brighton and on the edge of the Downs, described the 'finely situated' Hampton Lodge as 'elegant in its construction and commodious and spacious in all its appendages'. While such a description still held true by the time Chris Dyson's clients approached him about the house, it was in need of renovation as well as changes to its layout that would make it better suited to contemporary family life.

'I had known the clients for some time and they came to us because they had seen some of the work that we had done on Georgian buildings in Spitalfields,' says Dyson. 'They really liked our use of colour and the kind of adventurous approach we take to restoration but, given that they have two boys and a dog, they also wanted it to work as a family home. And it certainly has that feel about it now, with their mix of furniture and an art collection, including the pieces that they brought with them from their last house.'

The project encompassed the modernisation of the mansion itself, as well as an adjoining coach house and stable, while garden designer Andy Sturgeon was asked to work on the outside space, which includes a collection of mature trees. Inside, as well as updating services and utilities throughout, Dyson made several important changes in order to create a more informal, casual and family-friendly pattern of living. Chief among these was the decision to transform one of the more formal reception rooms into a combined kitchen and dining room. The resulting space is not only generously scaled, but also offers a strong sense of connection with the grounds, with views of the surrounding landscape through its sequence of floor-to-ceiling windows.

Left: Rear garden view.

'We introduced the wood-burning range, which has two hot plates and an oven, but most of the food prepping happens at the island, which is a bespoke piece with a marble top and an integrated sink,' Dyson says. 'There's also a separate pantry to one side of the kitchen with all the modern stainless-steel appliances, such as the dishwasher and fridge-freezer.'

The kitchen and dining room also offers a vibrant example of the characterful use of colour seen in all parts of the house. Here, architect and client opted for a specially mixed sky blue for the walls, along with a glossy mustard yellow for the ceilings that reflects the light and helps to lift the space. Custom lighting by Tom Singleton includes the statement piece over the dining table, while the mid-century dining chairs by Hans Brattrud contrast with period pieces of furniture, such as the chest of drawers nearby.

In the sitting room Dyson opted to carry the dark, moss-green colour used for the walls over to the window frames and shutters. Opting for an organic tone, rather than distracting white window frames, allows the eye a better chance of focusing on the views of the open landscape beyond the windows, which are one of the key delights of the house. Other bespoke touches here

Above left: Kitchen stove and oven.
Above right: Enfilade room, arrangement possible with jib door.

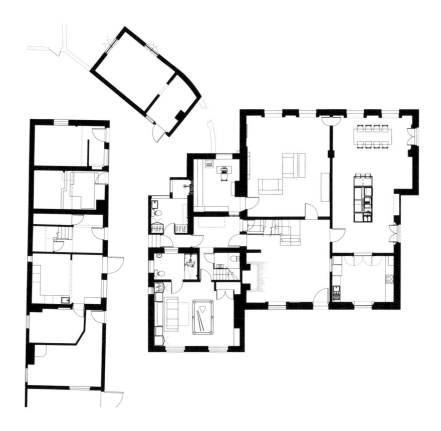

Ground floor

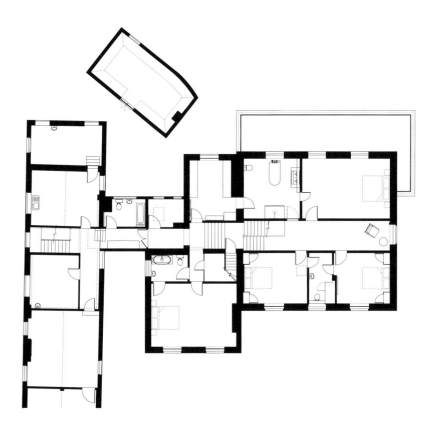

First floor

RESIDENTIAL: HAMPTON LODGE

Above left: First-floor corridor.
Above right: Master dressing room.
Left: Master bedroom.
Right: Master suite, enfilade arrangement.

include the exuberant ceiling rose, which was inspired by a design seen at Brighton Royal Pavilion. The family room has been painted an engaging mint green, while the custom joinery includes a hidden, fold-down bed that can be brought into use for guests as needed.

Upstairs, the focus on colour and pattern continues and includes the long landing, where paint suppliers March & Son mixed an orange-yellow sunshine tone while Dyson introduced a custom copper-pipe detail high on the walls to serve as a picture rail. For the master suite, colour and individuality are again key elements, with a potential bedroom alongside sacrificed to create a generously sized en suite bathroom, with a bespoke vanity and super-sized shower bay. A dressing room in arsenic green completes this appealing run of spaces for the parents.

A product of close collaboration with the clients, Hampton Lodge represents a key example of how the practice is able to combine architecture and interior design within one cohesive approach. 'I think we are great value in that respect', says Dyson, 'and as a practice we enjoy going down these rabbit holes with our clients and developing something that is unique to them.'

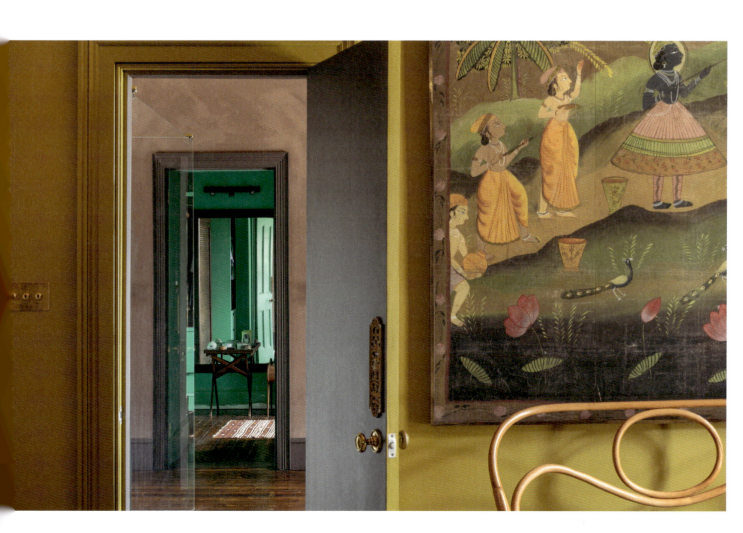

Wapping Pierhead, Wapping, London

Along with many other parts of East London, Wapping has experienced profound changes over the past century. This was once a thriving place of trade and commerce with merchants and their warehouses arranged around the docks and wharves, along with elegant terraces of Georgian and Victorian houses. During the Second World War, the area was badly damaged by bombing campaigns and subsequently the London Docks fell into decline and disuse, as shipping moved eastwards along the Thames and to the larger coastal ports.

Wapping Pierhead offers a striking example of such changes. Here, lines of terraced houses designed by the architect Daniel Alexander in 1811 once looked over an entrance to the London Docks and housed customs officers from the Dock Authority and their families. But after the destruction of the war years, parts of the dock system were infilled with rubble, including the space between the parallel streets of the Pierhead, which became a version of a garden square, but one that opened up towards the Thames. Later, the Pierhead was included within a conservation area intended to preserve the unique character and history of the riverside setting.

Such was the context of this project that sought to bring a fresh lease of life to a house at the end of one of these twin terraces, a property that had formerly been used as a convent but had then lain empty and unloved for several years. The owners, Tower Hamlets Council, had decided to put the building up for auction, partly because it had become structurally unsound, with a Victorian extension to one side beginning to pull away from the taller Georgian building alongside it, which is arranged over four storeys including a basement level.

Left: Rear garden view.

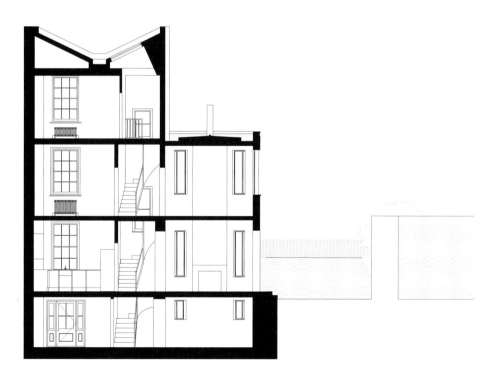

Left: Front of house.
Above right: Elevation frontage.
Below right: Cross section, old and new.

RESIDENTIAL: WAPPING PIERHEAD

Right: Rear garden elevation, new and old.
Below: Elevation, new extension.
Far right: New drawing room.

'It was originally a customs house for checking ships and cargo coming in and out of the London Docks,' says Dyson, 'but so much had changed over time. We looked at the house afresh and decided that from a structural point of view we really needed to replace the existing extension with something new that would help hold up this end of the terrace. But at the same time there was some space around the back of the house with a private walled garden, so we saw that there was also this opportunity to create more living space, which appealed to the clients, as they have two children.'

Dyson developed ideas for the new extension, drawing on various points of reference, both historical and modernist. The new addition has three levels, including a basement, while it also provides a fresh entrance to the street at ground level. Towards the rear, as it stretches into the back garden, the addition is rounded like the bow of a ship, echoing the shape of the period riverside houses nearby as they reach out towards the water. This curvaceous rear elevation adds an important sculptural dimension that softens the building, while the crafted brickwork also takes a degree of inspiration from the exterior of Louis Kahn's Exeter Library (1972), in New Hampshire, where the warmth, texture and artisanal quality of the brickwork adds an important layer to this dynamic composition. While the Pierhead extension is clearly modern, the use of brick also connects it materially and tonally to the original house alongside.

'The planning application won the hearts and minds of the conservation officer with a proposal that was modern but also paid a nod to the Georgian period in terms of the detailing,' says Dyson. 'We were terminating the terrace in one way, but we also wanted to make something that connected with the back garden, so the curved wall of the new sitting room at ground level is like a bay window in itself, with a series of framed openings looking out on to the walled garden.'

The new sitting room connects with the family living spaces in the original house, with an easy flow-through established to the dining room and kitchen alongside. The Georgian house was restored and modernised throughout, with period features retained wherever possible, while the first floor of the new extension provided space for an additional bedroom. The practice was also able to convert a small outbuilding in the rear garden into a pottery studio.

'The addition finishes the end of the terrace very nicely', says Dyson, 'especially with the roofline, where you have this original zigzag-shaped roof on the main house and then the curves of the extension. But the scale of the new part of the house is never overpowering, as it steps down towards the listed dock wall alongside it. For me, the human scale and human dimension is always very important, and being able to create spaces that people feel comfortable in. So there's a careful calibration here that takes the context into account but also the needs of the family.'

Right: Listed dockyard wall and new extension peeping over.

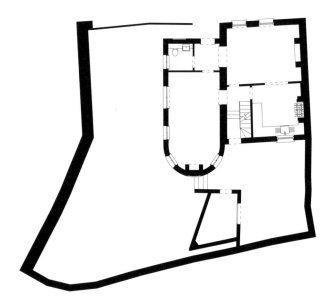

Ground floor

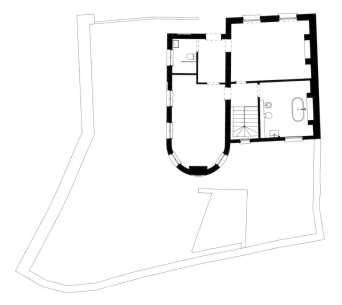

First floor

Mixed Use

One of the great strengths of Spitalfields, where Chris Dyson lives and works, is its diversity. The same is true of the neighbouring districts and neighbourhoods, where the palpable sense of energy and creativity within this part of London comes from the rich mixture of workplaces and housing, galleries and studios, retail and hospitality.

It is a place where Jane Jacobs' famous conditions for the 'generators of diversity' in our cities seem to be written clearly upon the streetscapes. Here, there is a blend of old and new, with buildings put to multiple and varied uses, combined with a healthy concentration of accommodation and amenities of all kinds. 'Cities have the capability of providing something for everybody, only because, and only when, they are created by everybody,' Jacobs wrote. 'The diversity, of whatever kind, that is generated by cities rests on the fact that in cities so many people are so close together, and among them contain so many different tastes, skills, needs, supplies, and bees in their bonnet.'

The successful revival of Spitalfields, Shoreditch and its neighbours over recent years seems to rest, in part, upon such diversity, with multiple ingredients combining to create a complex but dynamic mixture. Much of Chris Dyson's recent work has embraced opportunities to add to this diversity, particularly through the creation of mixed-use buildings and live-work spaces.

Left: Painted concrete panelling.

In some respects, Dyson's interest in mixed-use projects has been both encouraged and supported by a historical precedent for live-work buildings in this part of East London. The textile and garment industries, for example, have flourished here over the centuries within houses and workshops that sat hand in glove with the spaces people called home. Chris Dyson's own family house in Spitalfields (see p.31) once hosted a workwear micro-factory and, later, when Dyson updated the period building into a family home, he added office space to the rear of the property for his practice. When his practice then outgrew this live-work arrangement, it moved to the nearby Queen's Head (see p.93), a former pub that now serves as offices for Chris Dyson Architects but also holds a retail unit at street level currently occupied by a coffee shop.

Similarly, when Dyson was asked to work on the restoration and revival of the Sekforde public house in Clerkenwell (see p.99), the commission also involved a new-build addition alongside the historic pub providing both office and living space. Here, too, was a project that brought fresh diversity to the streetscape while revitalising a popular landmark and local amenity.

Another key thread within Dyson's mixed-use projects is that of the artist's home and studio. It is a creative way of working that has become well established in East London, with the practice enjoying collaborations with artists such as Michael and Oliver Chanarin (see p.107), as well as Philip and Charlotte Colbert, whose Maison Colbert is explored in more detail in the following chapter.

'The pleasure of working on projects with artists is that they want to do something unique and unusual that ties in with their way of seeing the world,' says Dyson. 'So for us, working on artists' homes and their associated working spaces has become something of a theme and one that we enjoy very much.' Increasingly, Dyson has also been exploring the live-work theme in other contexts. There is the example of the writer's retreat in the Cotswolds, known as the Gasworks, originally designed for Jeanette Winterson (see p.47), combining a home and two studies with a rural view. And in Suffolk, Dyson has designed a new multi-purpose studio alongside the period cottage shared with his wife and family (see p.121). Increasingly, diversity and variety enrich not only our cities but also the countryside.

Above left: Commercial Street offices of Chris Dyson Architects.
Above right: Cast-iron balustrades at Albion Works.

MIXED USE

Albion Works, Hackney, London

Following on from their successful collaboration on a live-work project in Spitalfields (see p.107), the Chanarin family and Chris Dyson reunited for a more ambitious project in Hackney. Once again, the project was to be mixed-use with a combination of commercial studio space and apartments, one of which is now occupied by the family.

With long experience in the world of property and architecture, painter Michael Chanarin and his son, photographer Oliver Chanarin, were tempted by the idea of working on a larger scale when a site in Hackney came up at auction. This backland property, which was owned by the local council, consisted of a derelict cabinet-making workshop and warehouse, dating back to the 19th century, along with later additions.

'The site, which was also used as a printworks, is surrounded by other buildings and has two access points at either end,' says Dyson. 'It's in a conservation area and the council eventually decided that they couldn't afford to restore it, so they decided to auction it to release money for other things, especially larger-scale housing. So the Chanarin family were the highest bidders and we started working on a design for the development, and managed to get it through the planning process within four months.'

The rapid pace of the design and planning application was all the more impressive given the complexities of the site itself and its surroundings, as well as the scale of the reconstruction required. The design itself was partly driven by issues related to privacy, light and orientation, with a need to sensitively navigate such questions not only for the benefit of potential residents of the new development but also for their neighbours.

Left: Entrance from Albion Drive.

West elevation

East elevation

Front elevation

Rear elevation

'The whole genesis of the plan was about looking east and west, rather than north and south, so as to respect the housing around the site,' says Dyson. 'It was a successful solution and really gave us our driving idea. Having studio space on the ground floor was also an important aspect for the planners, in that it retained some commercial use for the building rather than being entirely residential. So the whole ground floor is essentially commercial apart from the entrance to the five apartments above, which are spread over three floors.'

A great deal of thought was given to the layout of each of the individually designed apartments, taking into account sight lines, privacy and the need to connect with views of the surrounding gardens where possible. The fusion of new construction with the preserved remnants of the original buildings also allowed the practice to explore contrasting textures, which add to the richness of the exteriors and interiors.

A new concrete structural framework supports the entire building, but original brickwork has been retained where possible and supplemented by Petersen brick cladding, complete with blind windows at points where overlooking might be a concern. Timber shuttering for the poured concrete floor plates lends additional texture, especially in combination with the broad wooden floorboards that feature in the apartments. The practice designed kitchens and repeated elements for the five apartments, but in every case the designs and specifications needed to be tailored to the layout of each individual residence.

Above left: Gateway entrance from Albion Drive.
Above right: Living room subspace on first floor.
Right: Living room.

The collaborative process with the Chanarins extended to fixtures, fittings and detailing, with Oliver Chanarin designing some of the lighting for the apartments, for example. Graphic designer Tom Green, who is married to Oliver Chanarin's sister, was invited to collaborate on the design of the custom ironwork for the project, including the characterful access gateway that leads from the nearby street into the curtilage of the development.

'The family also wanted to be as sustainable as possible with the project,' says Dyson. 'So we have air source heat pumps, rainwater recycling and photovoltaic cells on the roof. The project is very progressive in that respect and the building is now incredibly efficient.'

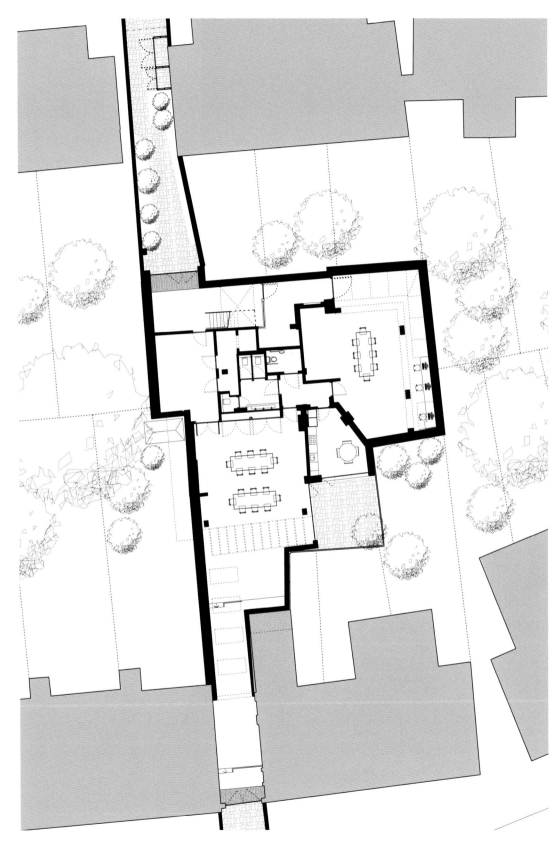

Ground floor

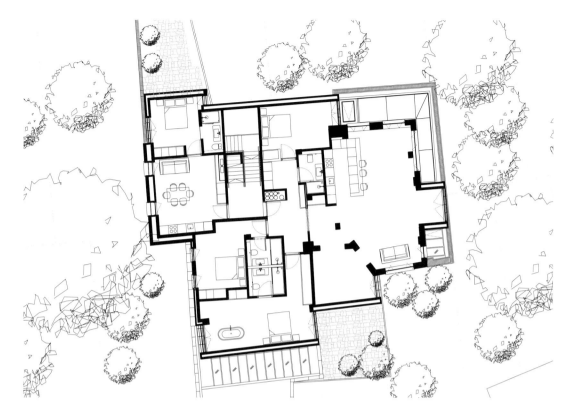

First floor

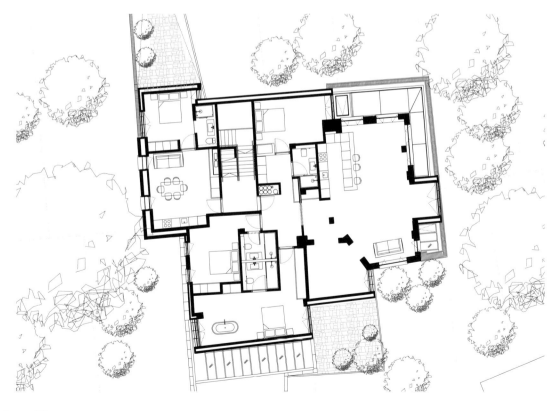

Second floor

MIXED USE: ALBION WORKS

Below: Albion Drive to Shrubland Road section.
Bottom: Cross section; studios at ground level, residential above.
Right: View up staircase shaft towards sky.

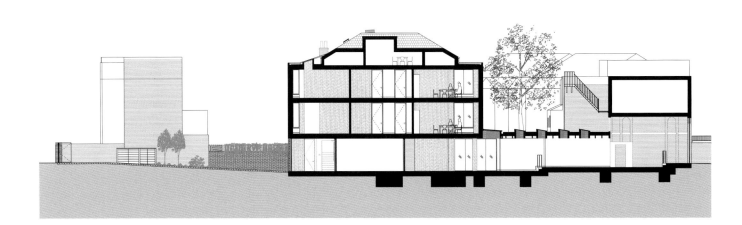

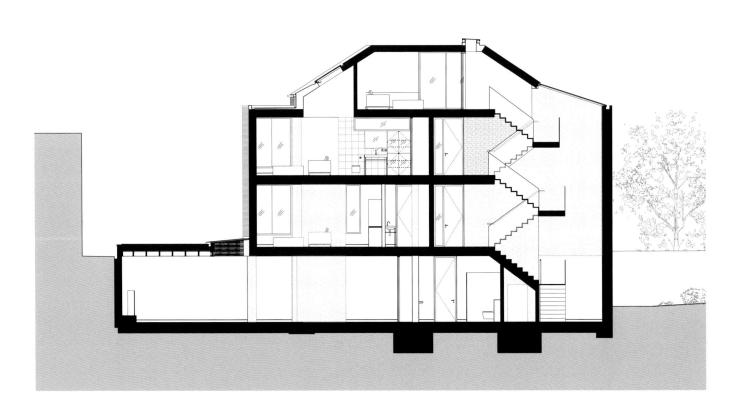

The Queen's Head, Spitalfields, London

For many years, Chris Dyson based his architectural practice within offices to the rear of his own Spitalfields home. But, eventually, the practice grew to a point where a significantly larger base was required but ideally within the same part of East London. Dyson took the decision to convert his old Princelet Street offices into an art gallery (see p.145) in 2016, and move the practice to its new home at the junction of Commercial Street and Fashion Street, giving the practice a presence on one of the key arterial roads running from Shoreditch towards Docklands.

'We are now a team of 20 architects with support staff, so we definitely needed more space,' says Dyson. 'So we found the Queen's Head, which was built as a pub in 1825 when they created Commercial Street by an act of parliament for safe passage of goods down to the London Docks. The pub was named after Queen Charlotte and when we took on the building we thought: this is wonderful, let's call it the Queen's Head again. We managed to find the old pub sign on the parapet and repainted it.'

More recently, the building had been used as offices and accommodation by the Bank of Bilbao. The traces of the old pub had largely been covered over and the entire building painted white, with all the original sash windows removed and replaced by uPVC inserts. Having uncovered the history of the former pub, Dyson and his team agreed to restore the building in a sympathetic manner that respected its past. At the same time, Dyson felt the prominent location was suited to a mixed-use blend of commercial space on the ground floor and offices for the practice above.

'We found some of the old tilework on the side of the building underneath a 1970s fascia,' says Dyson. 'So we restored the pub tilework with the help of Smith & Sons, who still make wonderful tiles in the traditional way, and they made these beautiful green-glazed, rectangular tiles for the exterior at ground-floor level, which complement the colours of "The Queen's Head" text that we restored.'

Left: Chris Dyson Architects' restored elevation for 1 Fashion Street and 74 Commercial Street.

For the ground floor, the practice created a spacious commercial unit, benefitting from its own access to Commercial Street and a neat run of Crittall windows and doors. The unit was originally used by tailor Timothy Everest and is now occupied by a coffee shop, suggesting the malleability of the space itself. There was also space a little further along Fashion Street for a separate entrance to the practice, as well as a dedicated meeting room for Chris Dyson Architects, known as 'The Queen's Room', supplemented by ancillary and service spaces down in the basement. The first and second floors now house the practice's offices, with space enough for between 12 and 16 staff on each storey.

'We invested a lot in the offices and the building but it's more than worth it because it's a showcase for our work,' says Dyson. 'Each floor of the offices consists of four rooms with a straight staircase connecting them and then we extended upwards to create a top floor with a staff kitchen space, topped by a central skylight, and then a roof terrace, which has this amazing view out over the City of London.'

Above left: Drawing of as-built Fashion Street elevation.

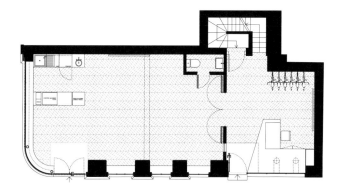

Ground floor

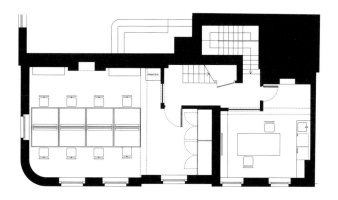

First floor

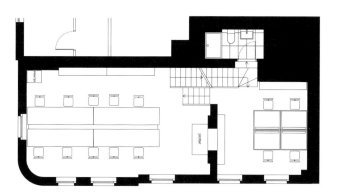

Second floor

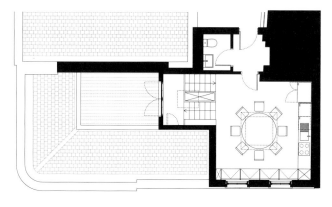

Third floor

MIXED USE: THE QUEEN'S HEAD

For Dyson and his family, the decision to create a sense of separation between work and home has also been beneficial. The short walk to the office each day creates a ritual that Dyson describes as 'healthy'.

'It was never good to have that feeling of the lights always burning back at home, which creates pressure in itself,' says Dyson. 'But also people sometimes like to come into the office at the weekends or out of hours to get things done and this new arrangement creates more freedom around those personal decisions in a way that might not have been the case when the office was in my backyard. But also the Queen's Head is a fabulous building to work in. It's narrow but full of light and the layout we have works really well for us. The restoration itself has been very rewarding as well and it feels as though the building has always looked like this in a way.'

Left: Meeting room, Fashion Street offices.
Below: The number 74 and the Queen's head mark the corner of Fashion Street and Commercial Street.

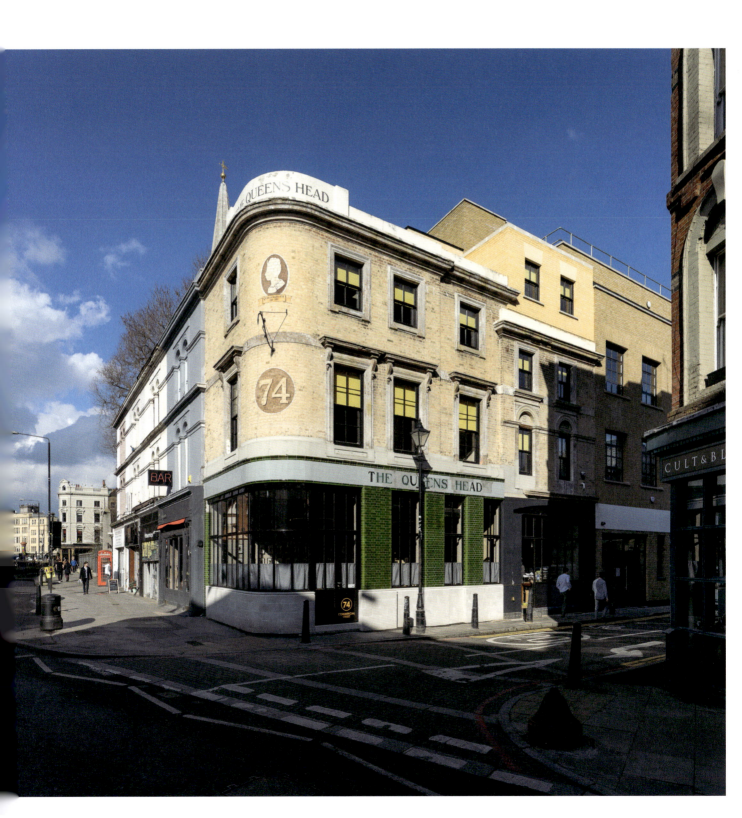

The Sekforde, Clerkenwell, London

The commission to work on the Sekforde in Clerkenwell embraced multiple elements. The key challenge was to sensitively restore and update the historic public house itself, with a particular emphasis on sustainable energy use and a green approach throughout. Beyond this, Chris Dyson Architects' client also asked the practice to design a new infill building alongside the pub, which now holds offices on the ground floor, plus a two-bedroom maisonette apartment on the first and second storeys above. This new addition needed to sit sympathetically with the pub, requiring a highly contextual yet contemporary design.

'The client, who is a barrister, came to us because he had seen some of our work in Spitalfields, including Albion Works (see p.83), which is also mixed-use,' says Dyson. 'He is very interested in architecture and likes to invest in buildings like this, partly because he is interested in how architecture can help to shape and improve people's lives.'

Dyson's client managed to acquire the freehold of the Sekforde and wanted to keep the pub running as a free house, while introducing additional public spaces, including a spacious restaurant and a welcoming function room. The project began with research on the history of the pub, which dates back to the Regency period, and the meticulous restoration of the exterior. Rendering over the brickwork was removed, and the brick washed and repointed, while the pub signage was recreated around the distinctive rounded end of the Sekforde, which sits at the triangular junction point of two adjoining roads.

Left: New and old at the Sekforde Arms, Sekforde Street.

At ground-floor level, the focus was on the restoration of the bar area, for which Dyson designed bespoke furniture, including the tables and chairs, as well as other integrated elements. A great deal of attention was paid to the colour choices in particular, demonstrating the practice's ongoing interest in selecting heritage colour palettes that also resonate within contemporary interiors.

'We chose colours with a Swedish influence but they were also influenced by our former neighbour in Spitalfields, Jocasta Innes, who produced this amazing book on Swedish interiors back in the 1990s,' Dyson says. 'We also collaborated on the project with the artist Ian Harper, who is another friend and neighbour, as well as master carpenter Matt Whittle, who made all the panelling for the exterior around the entrance and worked on the internal joinery. It was about bringing the pub back to life while keeping certain key elements like the old bar and the fireplace.'

Downstairs, Dyson dug downwards to create a more substantial and engaging basement dining area, with flagstone floors, exposed brickwork and a large mural at one end by Ian Harper depicting the Suffolk almshouses sponsored by the Elizabethan nobleman and philanthropist Thomas Seckford, after whom the pub and the nearby street are named. A glass floor plate here reveals some of the workings of the ground and water source heat pump that uses the subterranean springs of Clerkenwell as a source of both heating and cooling, as required.

Above left: Ground floor, pub interior.
Above right: Utilitarian basement steps.
Right: Basement cellar interior with heat exchanger in floor.

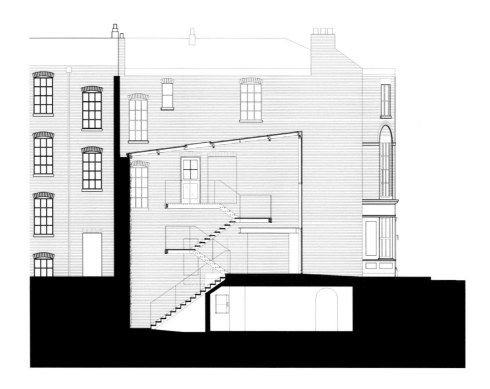

Upstairs, on the first floor, the practice converted a warren of rooms into what is now known as the 'ballroom', a multi-purpose function space, which can be used for dining, special events and meetings. Here again there was a thoughtful approach to the colour choices, with a lighter palette leading the eye upwards to a skyscape on the ceiling, which was also painted by Ian Harper, who studied at the Slade School of Fine Art and later began specialising in *trompe l'œil* and decorative paint finishes.

Right next door to the pub, Dyson designed a new building on a tight, triangular plot of land with a degree of separation provided by a recessed glass link that lightly ties the two buildings together. This new, three-storey addition is brick-faced and references the artisanal brickwork seen around Clerkenwell, yet the expression of the front elevation is clearly of the 21st century, featuring a neatly ordered grid of a dozen doors and windows with minimal but mindful detailing.

The design makes the most of the wedge-shaped site, drawing in light wherever possible, while respecting the neighbouring period buildings. This complementary infill project has provided additional live-work accommodation, adding to the character and vibrancy of the neighbourhood while also making use of a valuable but neglected micro site.

Left above: Corner elevation, new and old.
Left below: Section through new glazed circulation link.
Above: Sekforde Street south elevation.

MIXED USE: THE SEKFORDE

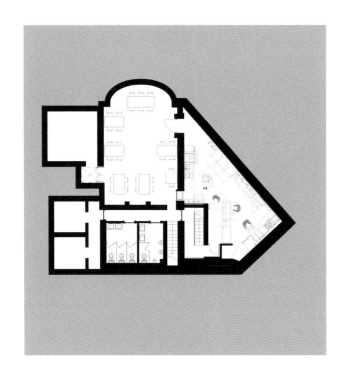

Basement

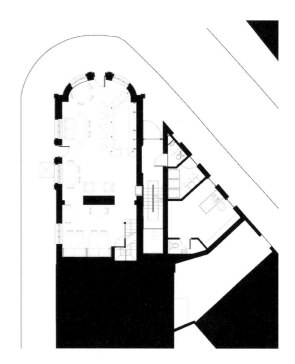

Ground floor

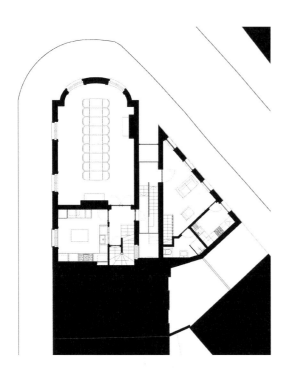

First floor

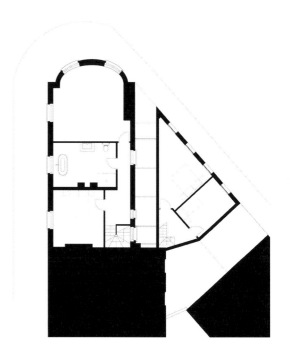

Second floor

Chanarin Residence & Studio, Spitalfields, London

Situated in the historic heart of Spitalfields, the Chanarin Residence & Studio offers a prime example of close collaboration between architect and artist, or artists. In this case, Chris Dyson's clients were a family of artists, principally the painter Michael Chanarin and his son, photographer Oliver Chanarin, as well as their wider family. They acquired an early-18th-century house close to Dyson's Spitalfields home, as well as a two-storey cottage to the rear situated just across a courtyard, then inhabited by a single mature fig tree.

'Unusually, there was a gate and driveway on the left-hand side of the Georgian house that was once used as a passage through to the courtyard,' says Dyson. 'Because of the passageway, there was never much depth to the Georgian house and no second set of rooms at the back of it, which you would normally see in Spitalfields. The ground floor of the house as it faces the street just had one room and a central staircase, as well as the gateway, and that was it. So a key part of the project was infill and making the most of the available space.'

The search for space, including areas for both living and working, took the practice in several different directions and encompassed the house, central courtyard and cottage. The Georgian residence itself required not only sensitive restoration but also extension to create a family home suited to Oliver Chanarin, his wife and their two children, as well as offering a substantial studio and gallery space.

Dyson secured planning permission to extend the house to the rear, while also digging down to create a new basement, adding another level to the four-storey building that was then connected with the original staircase. Family living spaces are situated at ground- and first-floor level, with five bedrooms positioned on various floors, including the former weaver's loft at the top of the building.

Left: Residence and studio overlooking garden.

By extending the building outwards into part of the rear courtyard, Dyson was able to create not only additional living space but also the new studio and gallery for the Chanarins. Accessed via the restored and remodelled gateway, this working space draws in light from a bank of glass looking over the courtyard garden, as well as a triptych of skylights over the part of the studio that pushes a little deeper into the hidden court. The rear of the building was then clad in an elegant timber coat while part of the new basement was devoted to an ancillary service space that complements the studio.

'Using steel framed construction at the back of the house, we were able to add a huge amount of volume, while restoring the original facade to the street,' says Dyson. 'You have the studio spaces over two floors but also there are now decent family living spaces for the residential part of the building, so it was a transformative project.'

Right: Front room at Princelet Street, left in a state of disrepair.

Princelet Street elevation.

New rear elevation finished in cedar cladding.

TWO HOUSES ONE PLOT
SHARE ONE COURTYARD
AND A FIG TREE.

Chris, 2009

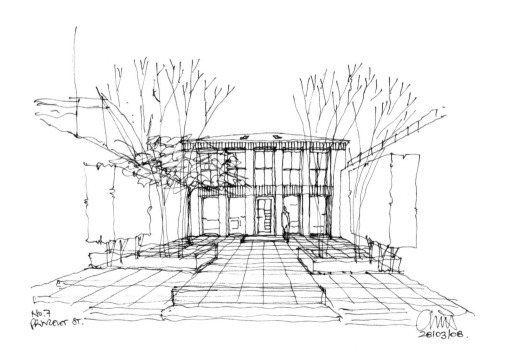

NO. 7
PRINCES ST.

Chris
28/03/08

The secret courtyard garden not only draws in light and air, but became an engaging outdoor room shared with the cottage to the rear. Once described as a kind of 'dower house' for the older generation of the family, the Victorian cottage, which is arranged over two storeys, has also been fully updated and revived. The ground floor is devoted to a semi-open-plan living area, while the upstairs is now a spacious master suite, with both levels enjoying views of the garden via an ordered set of five windows and doorways over two levels, ensuring that the cottage also feels light and bright.

'The combination of the different generations of the family, along with live-work, made this a really lovely and rewarding project,' says Dyson. 'Eventually the family decided to move on to another collaboration with us, Albion Works (see p.83), but they kept hold of this property and it's now rented out. The flexibility of the design can be seen in the way that it's been successfully adopted by new tenants.'

Left above: Exploded axiometric sketch.
Left below: Sketch of rear courtyard view of cottage.
Above: Bedroom to bathroom.
Above right: Bedroom to bathroom across staircase.

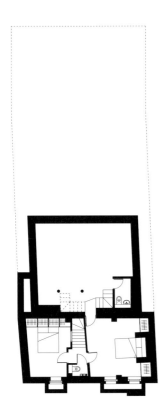

Basement

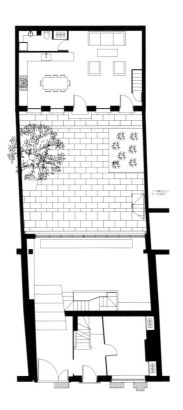

Ground floor

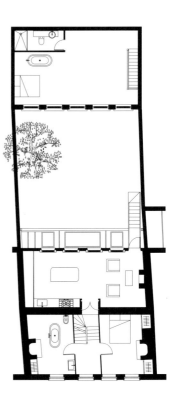

First floor

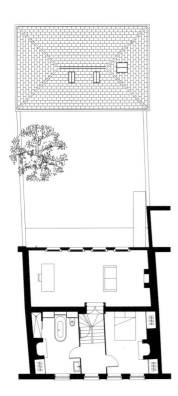

Second floor

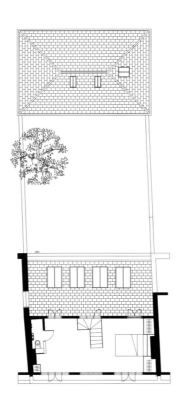

Third floor

Right: Master bedroom view from former weaver's loft.

Timothy Everest Store, Shoreditch, London

Both Shoreditch and neighbouring Spitalfields have a long relationship with the garment industry. Historically, this part of East London was once a hub for fashion wholesalers and retailers, with some of this heritage and its legacy still visible on the streetscape. In many cases, such businesses sat on the ground floor of houses with living space above, creating a strong precedent for a live-work model in this part of the city. Stepping back even further, Spitalfields was known as the 'silk district' in the 18th century, when Huguenot weavers settled here, with their looms sharing space with their families in the same Georgian buildings.

Chris Dyson Architects have been drawn towards the rich narrative of the neighbourhood's garment industry on various occasions. Some years ago, in 2004, they were asked to design the interiors of a concept store on Fournier Street for the American shoe and apparel company Timberland. Rather than embracing the corporate look of many such stores, the experimental Fournier Street shop reflected an ambition to create a more subtle and contextual design in keeping with the neighbourhood itself.

More recently, the practice was asked by tailor and fashion designer Timothy Everest to design the interiors of a concept store on Redchurch Street, which sits on the vibrant borderland between Shoreditch and Spitalfields. The space in question is on the ground floor of a mixed-use building dating back to the 1950s, with retail at street level and a series of apartments above.

Here, Dyson balanced multiple reference points and sources of inspiration. There was the garment industry heritage outlined above and the way Timothy Everest, who spent many years working in this part of London, connected with this history. But there was also the semi-industrial character of the 1950s building itself, which helped to guide and inform the project.

Left: Exterior view of shopfront by vPPR architects.

'We wanted to connect the Timothy Everest culture with the idea of Redchurch Street being a setting for workshops and fabrication in the 19th and 20th centuries,' says Dyson. 'But at the same time these are interiors that need to work in the 21st century, so we decided to adopt a slightly more industrial aesthetic while making bespoke but flexible fittings using copper piping and brass, which means that displays and rails of clothes can be moved around very easily as the collection evolves.'

The shop frontage, inserted into the 1950s facade, manages to encapsulate a handful of themes and references. The cast-iron latticework above the window glazing recalls lacework and sheets of fabric, while the bobbin door handle also references the area's history. Internally, the practice was able to make good use of a partial basement to the rear of the unit, which created space enough for a mezzanine level, with a more intimate tailoring and fitting space slotted beneath.

The treatment of textures and materials splices a semi-industrial quality, with Everest's own interest in Japanese culture and design reflected in the minimalism of the detailing but also the way – for instance – one's eye is drawn right through the shop towards a large window framing a view of the simply planted courtyard garden to the back of the building. The custom wall panelling seen to the rear of the shop was spray-painted with a surface concrete finish by cabinetmaker turned decorative artist Leigh Cameron, creating an engaging fusion of period referencing and the industrial, as also seen in the panelling around the false fireplace in the lower-level fitting room, which features a herringbone floor.

'We also worked on the lighting design and, as with the Timberland store, we painted out the ceiling and installed the lighting rigs on the ceilings, with the idea that the mood could be changed through the lighting according to the time of day,' says Dyson. 'There is almost a sense of domesticity about the furniture and fittings in the store but when you are dealing with a commercial fit-out you do need a certain degree of drama. Creating that sense of theatre is really important to make the shop attractive enough for people to want to come in and enjoy it.'

Right above: Sketch of interior from street.
Right below: Sketch of interior view of split levels of shop.

TIMOTHY EVEREST STORE
REDCHURCH STREET. E1.

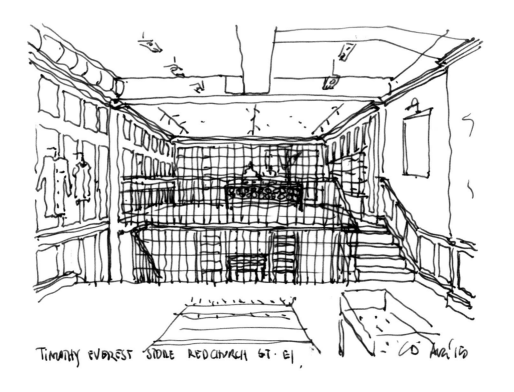

TIMOTHY EVEREST STORE REDCHURCH ST. E1

MIXED USE: TIMOTHY EVEREST STORE

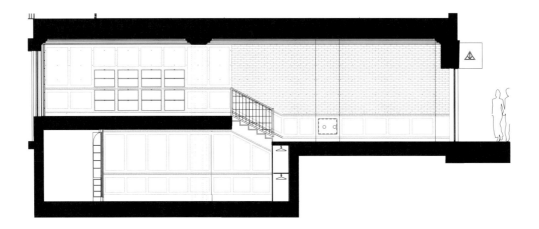

Cross section

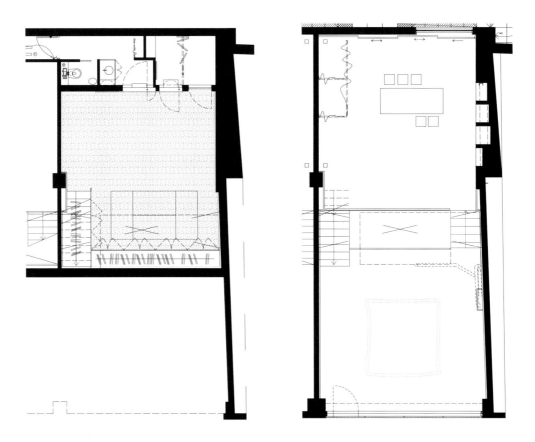

Lower plan

Upper plan

Architect's Home & Studio, Preston St Mary, Suffolk

Together with the rest of his family, Chris Dyson has enjoyed spending time in Suffolk for many years. The relationship began with weekend visits and holidays but eventually developed into a greater commitment, especially after his parents moved from Yorkshire to East Anglia, while his sister also settled nearby. Eventually, the opportunity arose to buy a house in the village of Preston St Mary and so Dyson and his wife Sarah decided to purchase their rural retreat.

'It made a lot of sense for us,' says Dyson, 'and not only because of the family ties. We can actually get here from Spitalfields in around an hour and a half and be in this completely different and very relaxing environment, with greenery all around us and open countryside nearby, and the big, open skies. I soon realised that I'm not alone in loving the county and that there are quite a few architects and artists who live in this area for similar reasons.'

The Suffolk house was first offered to them by a friend and neighbour in Spitalfields, who had taken the difficult decision to sell up. Knowing that the Dysons were fond of East Anglia, he offered them the keys to the house and suggested that they take a look. The temptation proved too much to resist.

'It's a Grade II listed house, which is thatched and dates back to at least the 17th century,' Dyson says. 'Before that, we think there was a barn on the site that was then converted into two adjoining houses, with some overlap between the two. So, when it was first built, there would have been nothing around it but a stream and open fields, with all the neighbouring houses along the lane coming later.'

**Left: Garage and studio door.
Page 122, clockwise from top left: Drawing room, study, daybed in library, bedroom.
Page 123: View of kitchen garden, new and old thatch.**

By acquiring part of an adjoining garden, the family were able to make space for vegetable beds and a verdant private realm to the rear of the property. Beyond this, Dyson began thinking about plans to extend the house, and then design and build a studio on the site of a former garage on the other side of the garden.

The first challenge was to tidy up the back and side of the house itself, which had been compromised by an extension and a failing conservatory. Given the slope in the rear garden, Dyson decided to design a new timber-framed garden room raised above ground level on a platform supported by four brick piers. This largely glass-sided pavilion, with a fireplace on one side, now serves as a spacious dining room as well as somewhere to enjoy the garden views. This new pavilion is tied to the rest of the house via a fresh entrance hallway, which also connects to a new brick-vaulted kitchen

Above: The house in context.
Right, clockwise from top left: East face of garden room, west face of garden room, garden room looking north, garden room interior.

that replaced a former coal store and lean-to; a skylight was added over the hallway to brighten the spaces around it.

'Creating the walled garden was also a lot of work but a real joy,' says Dyson. 'As well as the vegetable garden and flower beds, we have a Cor-Ten-coated shed and then a shepherd's hut that my daughter Isabella, who is an artist, uses as a painting studio when she is here.'

The most recent addition to the house has been the multi-purpose studio, which is also timber-framed and timber-clad but modestly scaled and compact, sitting on the footprint of a garage that once held just enough space for two cars arranged end to end. Working within these restrictions, Dyson was able to design an elegant studio building, which is largely on one level and offers a framed view of the garden at one end.

Left: Studio annexe garden access.
Above left: Studio interior.
Above right: Studio shower and bathroom.

Internally, the studio offers a flexible and open working space that enjoys the garden vista. The other end of the building, which faces the driveway and nearby lane, is a masterclass in space maximisation, including a compact galley kitchen, a shower room and a mezzanine that mean the studio can also be used as a guest lodge by visiting friends and family. The new studio, along with the garden room and kitchen, has been transformative in terms of contemporary family living yet these additions have not detracted from the intrinsic character of the listed house.

'We like the house and garden very much, but we also find the area very liberating,' says Dyson. 'We have made friends here and it's such a great contrast to being in London. You are so much more aware of the seasons here and the way that the landscape changes over time with the choice of crops planted in the fields. It's also a quiet place to work, although having said that I would never give up the office or working face to face. There's something very valuable about collaborating with people in the social environment of the office.'

Culture & Community

Left: Gallery to the rear of Princelet Street, steel stair to basement.

Over the course of many years, architect Chris Dyson has expressed his commitment to the culture and community of his own London neighbourhood, Spitalfields, in various ways. His connections to the art world, in particular, were forged in this part of East London and have resulted in much-valued friendships and collaborations with artists, makers and artisans. More recently, Dyson's practice has expanded far beyond its heartland to explore cultural projects and commissions in very different contexts while exhibiting a similar understanding of the needs of specific communities and a wish to adopt a collaborative approach founded on creative dialogues.

One of the most personal expressions of Dyson's interest in the art world was the creation and curation of his own gallery, Eleven Spitalfields (see p.145). Dyson and his wife Sarah created their bespoke art space in a dedicated building to the rear of the family home in Princelet Street, Spitalfields (see p.31). Top-lit and with significant wall space organised over two levels, Eleven Spitalfields offered Dyson and his family fresh opportunities to engage with local artists and the wider creative community. In doing so, Dyson was able to reinforce relationships with artists such as Adam Dant, Mona Hatoum, Martin Richmond, Jock McFadyen RA, Richard Wilson RA and Ian Harper, who have collaborated with the practice on various projects.

Most recently, Dyson and Dant worked together on a competition-winning entry for a new cultural and exhibition space on Brick Lane known as Bishopsgate Goodsyard. Arranged over five levels, this significant new community hub has been designed to provide exhibition galleries, along with a multi-purpose events space and artisanal studios; in doing so, the project encapsulates many of the concerns closest to Dyson's heart.

Also in Spitalfields, Dant contributed artwork and branding to Chris Dyson Architects' headquarters for Confer & Karnac (see p.161) on Strype Street. Here, Dyson designed a bookshop combined with administrative spaces for two publishing imprints, an events space and a recording studio. At the same time, the brief also encompassed flexible spaces suited to hosting a rotating programme of art exhibitions, adding to the cultural life of the neighbourhood while offering an important platform to contemporary artists.

Just around the corner from Confer & Karnac, Dyson worked closely with artists Philip and Charlotte Colbert on the creation of an ambitiously scaled and beautifully executed live-work space. Encompassing studio and office spaces for the two artists and their teams on the lower floors, Maison Colbert (see p.135) also involved the design of a new family residence across the upper storeys of this radically reimagined building.

Above: Entrance to cultural building from King's Square.
Right: Maison Colbert Gallery, ground floor.

While Chris Dyson Architects' engagement with Spitalfields and East London continues, at the same time commissions have taken them further afield. There is, for example, the Crystal Park Café (see p.151), which provides a much-needed amenity set within the context of Joseph Paxton's famous Victorian pleasure gardens. A new-build project designed in response to a very particular setting, the café is not only a place of refreshment but a vibrant social hub, with a dedicated events space on the upper storey of this new landmark within the park.

The practice is also working on a new teaching building for Harrow Arts Centre in North London. Here, Dyson has replaced a handful of temporary teaching cabins with a contextual new building holding three new teaching spaces plus a collection of eight new studios, which will be available for rent by local artists.

Above: Drawing by Chris Dyson of Crystal Palace Park Café.
Right: Rendering by DRAW a HALF-CIRCLE of Harrow Arts Centre, Greenhill Building.

The design references the surrounding buildings of the arts centre, yet its form and expression are clearly contemporary, with its saw-tooth roofline punctuated by skylights that draw sunlight deep into the studio spaces.

'Rather like the Crystal Palace Park project, Harrow Arts Centre is very community-focused,' says Dyson. 'In fact, one led to the other in that Harrow saw what we had done in South London and it led to this. The services and spaces that Harrow provides for the community are seriously in demand with people who want to practise music and dance, paint or follow all sorts of other creative pursuits. The local council is very rightly proud of its achievements at Harrow Arts Centre and the new rental studios, especially, will provide another income stream to help support the growth of the campus.'

Maison Colbert, London

There is a strong tradition in East London of living above the shop. It is a pattern of living and working that has continued through into the 21st century and has resulted, in certain instances, in some extraordinary and unique buildings. Such is the case with Maison Colbert, where the idea of living above the shop has been revisited and reinterpreted on an ambitious scale.

The Maison Colbert project provides gallery space and offices for two artists, Philip Colbert and Charlotte Colbert, who are husband and wife but work independently of one another. The Colberts' private family residence, shared with their two young children, is arranged over three dedicated floors above these new and bespoke workspaces.

'The Colberts were looking for space for their own studios, a gallery and a home in either central or East London,' says Chris Dyson. 'Then we happened upon a row of five derelict terraced houses in this amazing location right on the edge of the City, which was a sound investment. After looking at lots of other possibilities, the Colberts eventually made an offer for these five Victorian houses, with a row of former shops at street level.' Each of these shops was narrow – little more than four metres (13 feet) wide – which had limited both their use and appeal. Working closely with the Colberts, Dyson and his practice developed ideas for essentially rebuilding the property behind the existing facade in order to create what is, in effect, a new building behind the period frontage where spaces are liberated, volumes expanded and natural light introduced throughout.

Left: Basement gallery, Maison Colbert.

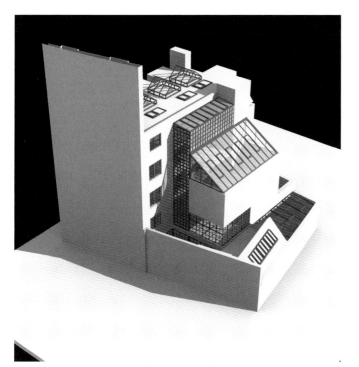
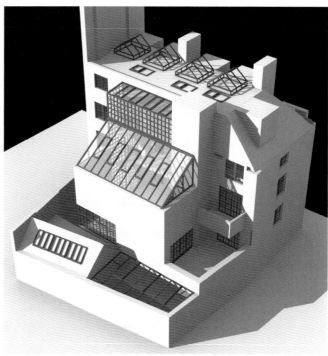

Left above: Chris Dyson Architects' model of Maison Colbert.
Above: Massing models of Maison Colbert.

'The whole idea of Maison Colbert is quite unique,' Dyson says. 'Philip and Charlotte Colbert have been able to stamp their artistic authority on the project, and we have also managed to make a great piece of architecture and design. It is no longer five properties, but this very spacious and flexible live-work space, which offers them all kinds of possibilities as to how they decide to use it.'

The original brick facade of the building to the street was preserved, restored and revived, including the run of shopfronts and the pattern of fenestration. Beyond this, the practice dug down to create a new basement level, as well as pushing into a former landlocked courtyard at the back of the site. During this major excavation process, Roman remains were discovered, which led to an archaeological dig that spanned six months. The new basement proved essential to the creation of a double-height studio and gallery, suited to the creation and curation of artworks and sculptures by both Philip and Charlotte Colbert. There are also office, administration and meeting rooms at both ground- and first-floor levels, including production spaces for Charlotte Colbert, whose portfolio of work now includes feature films.

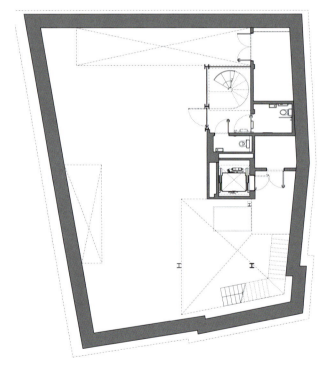

Above: Spiral staircase.
Above right: Rear staircase to basement.
Right: Basement gallery plan.

138

The family's private residence, which can be accessed independently of the workspaces below, was designed in conjunction with the Colberts, and interior designers Angus and Charlotte Buchanan of Buchanan Studio. The residential part of the project encompasses generously scaled living spaces, a planted terrace and conservatory, four family bedrooms and an additional one-bedroom apartment. Inspiration for the interiors included not only themes drawn from the artists' own work but also landmark art hotels and artists' retreats. The resulting aesthetic is luxurious and sometimes theatrical, but also sophisticated and original.

'The reference points included Charleston in East Sussex, La Colombe d'Or in the South of France and the Le Meurice Hotel in Paris, all of which connect with the art world,' says Dyson. 'But at the same time this is also the Colberts' family home and feels that way, because they have shaped it. But the building also has the potential to evolve and to host exhibitions and events, among other uses. As artists, the Colberts will want to direct how the building will be used over time. They have given it a lot of love, care and attention to detail.'

Above: Drawing room.
Right above: Entrance to drawing room.
Right below: Entrance from conservatory into the family drawing room and kitchen.

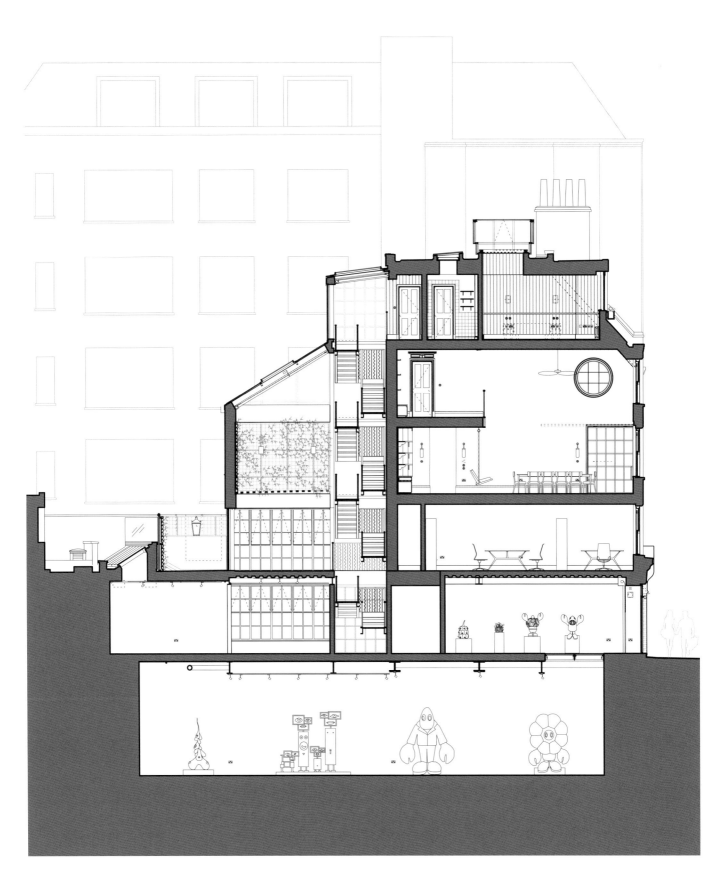

While the transformation of the building has been radical, its sense of character as it faces the streetscape has been respected. Visible new additions, such as the mansard and dormer level at the top of the terrace, have been subtly designed and the sense of a shopfront, or rather a collection of shopfronts, is still clearly visible.

'You can still read the five shops and houses,' says Dyson. 'The project has definitely embraced the character of the streetscape and set a standard for the rest of the block to match in the way that we have restored the frontage, corbels and signage. Not many clients would invest in these things, but they became an important part of the project. You can step through these shopfronts into an amazing new gallery space and all that goes with it.'

Left: Street cross section of gallery and dwelling.
Above right: Circulation, winter garden.

Eleven Spitalfields Gallery, Spitalfields, London

'We believe that creative space is extremely valuable to society,' wrote Chris Dyson and his wife Sarah in their book *Compendium* (2016). 'It provides the necessary vessel in which the soul and fabric of a city can flourish. Every city must foster a creative quarter, whatever the size, to enrich people's lives. In this way we will ensure that London is a city of cultural distinction in the fields of art and design. The rest will, and usually does, follow . . .'

The book was published by the Dysons to celebrate the first eight years running their own gallery, Eleven Spitalfields, and the work of many of the artists who had exhibited there. They included painters, photographers, textile designers and sculptors, along with artists that Chris Dyson has collaborated with, in one way or another, on various architectural and interiors projects, including Adam Dant, Michael Chanarin and Ian Harper. Many of these exhibitors are closely related to East London, yet the gallery has also offered space to artists from much further afield, including the French photographer Christine Bergougnous and the Scotland-based artist Patricia Cain.

The idea of a family-run gallery began with two elegant, timber-panelled rooms on the ground floor of the Dysons' own family home on Princelet Street. From the beginning, Chris Dyson decided that a multi-purpose, live-work arrangement would work well within the early-18th-century building that he thoughtfully restored and updated (see p.31), with communal exhibition and work spaces at street level, and the Dysons' private living spaces above. As well as serving as occasional meeting rooms, these two

Left: Gallery at rear of 11 Princelet Street.

ground-floor rooms were ideally suited to exhibitions, sitting on an axis of circulation that connected not only with the main entrance hallway but also with the offices of Dyson's practice, which he designed and built on the site of a former joinery workshop to the rear of the property. The couple shared the curation of the gallery, savouring opportunities to collaborate on events and projects with a wide range of contributing artists.

'Through the gallery we have met a great number of friends and artists,' says Dyson. 'They have guided us in the curation of several of the shows and also introduced us to their friends. Into this soup then comes Spitalfields as a place of immigration and creativity; artists feel comfortable here and often inspired by the place.'

Eventually, an opportunity arose to expand the gallery. Dyson's practice outgrew the studio to the rear of the house and moved to fresh offices at the Queen's Head (see p.93), which is just five minutes' walk away. The empty studio was perfectly suited for use as an exhibition space, being top-lit by a substantial lantern and largely arranged as an open space at ground-floor level, with ancillary and service areas at the far end. The Dysons then decided to create an additional floor by excavating downwards, below the studio, to create a complementary basement level. To ensure that the basement would be adequately lit and suitably welcoming, Dyson carved out a light well right at the centre of the studio, directly below the roof lantern, which allows natural light to circulate down to the lower floor.

The enlarged Eleven Spitalfields gallery offered the Dysons a significant increase in wall space that was well suited to the display of larger artworks. The walls were painted a crisp white with flooring in white terrazzo, adding to the quality and character of the space. Elements such as the new folded steel staircase down to the basement display area were designed to maximise the perception of space and volume without distracting from the overall purity of the interiors.

As demonstrated by the example of seminal exhibition spaces such as Sir John Soane's Dulwich Picture Gallery, the use of toplight is ideally suited to the display of art and this proved to be the case with Eleven Spitalfields. From its small beginnings, this family-run space and cultural 'vessel' became a valuable addition to the neighbourhood, playing its own part in encouraging the creative life of the community. At the same time, the gallery remained a personal and formative project for the Dyson family.

'We chose the work that we exhibited based entirely on what we inherently like,' says Dyson. 'For us as art collectors, and for me as an architect, Eleven Spitalfields was a natural extension of our shared passion for art, architecture and the community we live in.'

Above: Gallery at rear of 11 Princelet Street.
Above right: Gallery interior.
Right: Steel staircase to basement.

CULTURE & COMMUNITY: ELEVEN SPITALFIELDS GALLERY

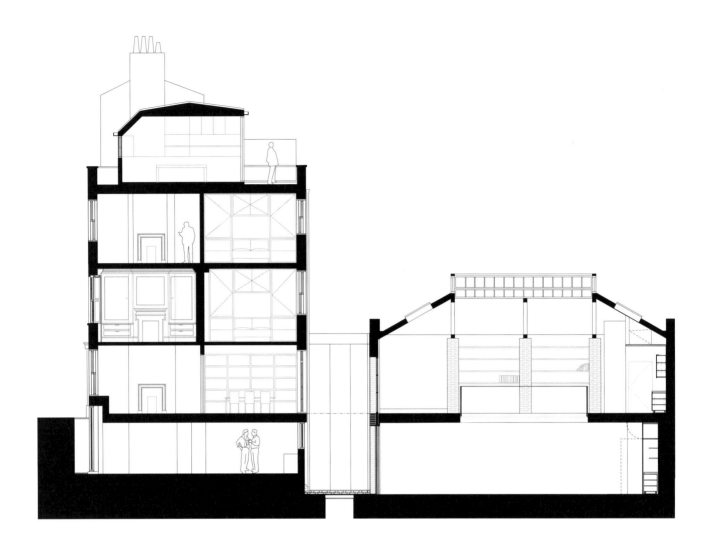
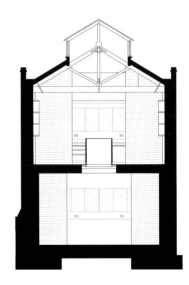

Above: Long section through house and gallery.
Right: Long section through house and gallery.
Far right: Toplight into basement.

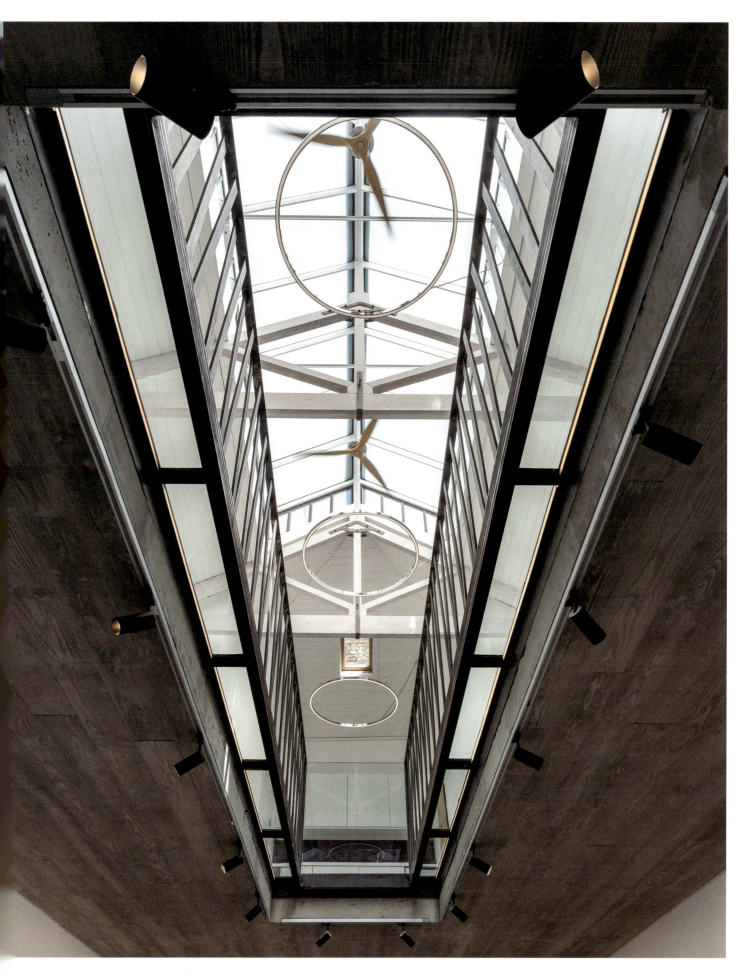

Crystal Palace Park Café, Bromley, London

One of the great Victorian pleasure grounds, Crystal Palace Park remains a much-loved green space for the communities that encircle it. The mature trees and planting give the parkland here a semi-rural feel, yet this is also a place rich in history and the imprint of lost buildings. The park was, of course, the site of Joseph Paxton's Crystal Palace, which was originally built in Hyde Park for the Great Exhibition of 1851 and subsequently reconstructed at its new home in Sydenham Hill. The parkland around the Palace was laid out by Paxton and his associates, with contributions to the site from – among others – Isambard Kingdom Brunel, who designed and built two water towers that sat at either end of the great glasshouse.

When the building was destroyed by fire in 1936, many traces were left behind and can still be seen within the park. These include the terraces on which the Palace once sat; a collection of dinosaurs by sculptor Benjamin Waterhouse Hawkins; and thoroughfares through the trees that populate and punctuate the parkland itself. Later, Crystal Palace Park became a key sporting venue, home to cricket, football and then the National Sports Centre, while also hosting a concert bowl. In 1986, the London Borough of Bromley became the custodians of the park and began a lengthy process of consultation and re-evaluation, seeking to balance the historical legacy of the parkland with the need to provide the community with not just valuable green space but also a suitable range of amenities that would carry Crystal Palace Park well into the 21st century.

One of the most recent additions is the Crystal Palace Park Café, designed by Chris Dyson Architects, and now managed and run by the local café company Brown & Green. The new building was commissioned by the Borough of Bromley to replace a former café here dating back to the 1950s, which had reached the end of its natural life, with the project assisted by a £2 million funding contribution from the Mayor of London. Naturally, the project began with a detailed research stage looking into the extraordinary context of the site and setting.

Left: The café in the context of the lakeside.

'There is clearly this amazing history to the park, which is Grade II* listed on the Register of Historic Parks and Gardens,' says Dyson. 'We were originally invited to partner on a bid for the project as conservation architects in association with Kinnear Landscape Architects, who were also working on some other improvements to the park, including an upgrade to some of the play areas. We were asked to concentrate on the café, which was looking very tired but was also tucked away and quite difficult to find. So we wanted to design a building with a more significant profile that could be seen and found more easily from within the park itself.'

The new, two-storey café sits close to the central axial line, established by Paxton himself, which carries through the parkland and past the sports stadium towards the terraces that once hosted the Crystal Palace. Working with Lynn Kinnear, Dyson's practice established a quartet of fresh pathways that easily connect with Paxton's route to one side and also – via a bridge at the first-floor level of the new building – with a walkway towards the boating lake on the other side of the café.

'A lot of investment went into the pathways and adjusting the landscaping, as well as bringing in new services to the building,' says Dyson. 'It is very easy to find now but the other part of this was creating a more distinctive architectural form that could be seen within the park, especially the pitched roof and the tall chimney. We invested a lot of time in form-finding and were thinking of trying to connect in some way with the Waterhouse Hawkins dinosaurs that sit within the park and are also listed. In the end, we honed in on the idea of a dinosaur's skin and translated that into the cedar scales that are on the exterior walls and the roof of the new building.'

Above: Aerial view.
Right: Paxton axis elevation.

Above: Sun terrace outside café.
Right: Conceptual doodle of the building.
Right above: Timber shingles and brick detail.

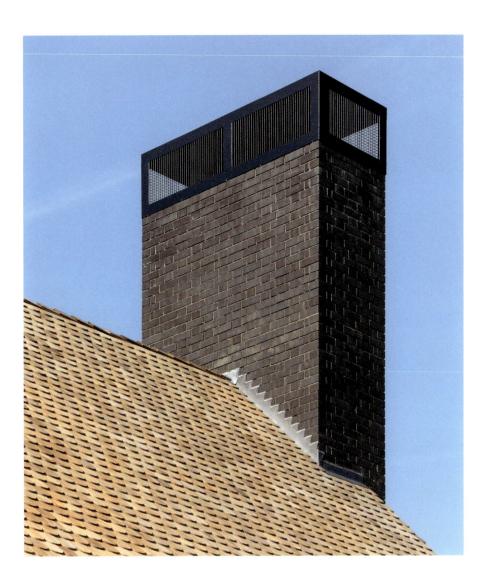

The contextual referencing to Hawkins and Paxton is subtly done, fusing with a barn-like outline that also sits well among the mature trees all around the building and the boating lake, offering a landscape that is almost bucolic in character. Dyson decided to use a structural steel framework for the building, which was then super-insulated and clad in the timber shingles, which have rounded, scale-like tips. These contrast neatly with the brickwork of the tall chimney that anchors one gable end while forming a high beacon that can be seen right across the park.

The ground-floor café looks out on to an adjoining terrace, which forms a fresh-air extension of the spaces within, and offers outdoor tables and seating. Upstairs, Dyson created a flexible event room with views out over the parkland while open ceiling trusses add to the overall sense of space and volume. At one end, the event room leads out on to an elevated, balconied terrace with further seating of its own and then, from here, to the bridge that leads towards the raised banks of the boating lake.

CULTURE & COMMUNITY: CRYSTAL PALACE PARK CAFÉ

Paxton axis elevation

Cross section

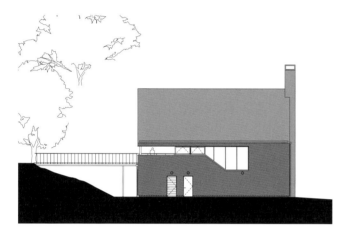

Long elevation

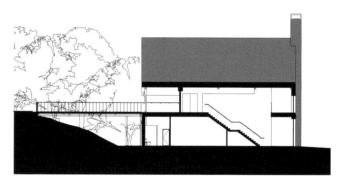

Staircase section to lakeside

'The brief was for a ground-floor café that can used by everybody during the day, including dog walkers and cyclists, with bike racks provided alongside the terrace,' says Dyson. 'And then the events room upstairs is this barn-like volume that can be used for yoga classes, dancing, birthday parties and other special events. But importantly, the building doesn't really have a back to it and every elevation invites you to come and visit. From the height and form, you know where it is, and you can say that from all views and perspectives it's a handsome addition to the park.'

'This marks the biggest investment by the Mayor in a borough-run park in a decade,' said London Deputy Mayor for Planning, Regeneration and Skills, Jules Pipe, at the opening of the café in 2019. 'I'm sure this will become a popular attraction for locals and visitors.'

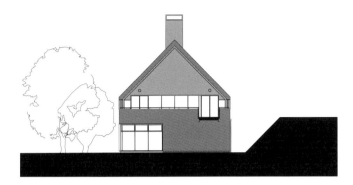

Lakeside elevation

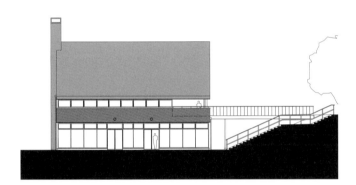

Terrace elevation and bridge to lakeside

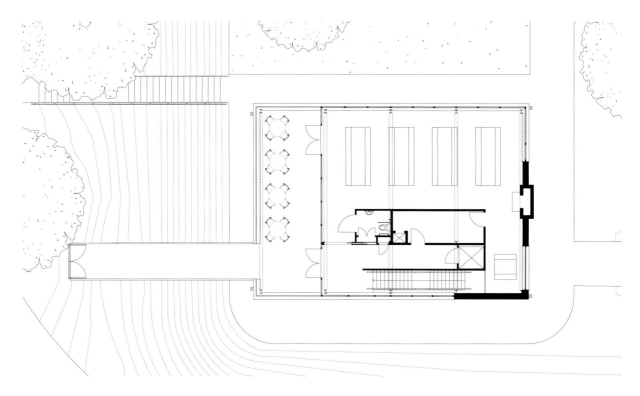

Lakeside plan level

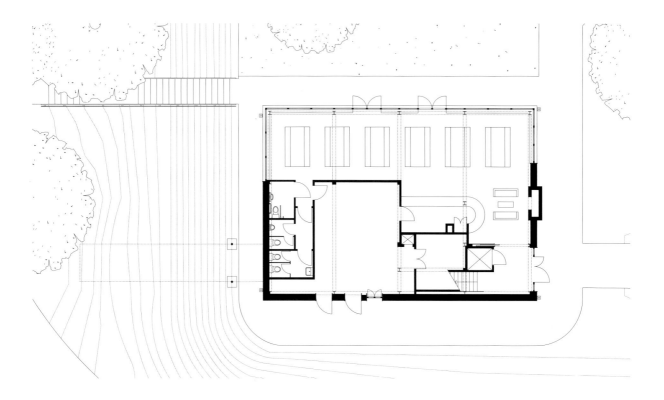

Park level entrance plan

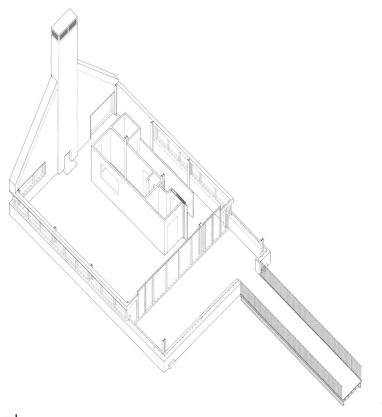

Axiometric drawing of lakeside level and bridge

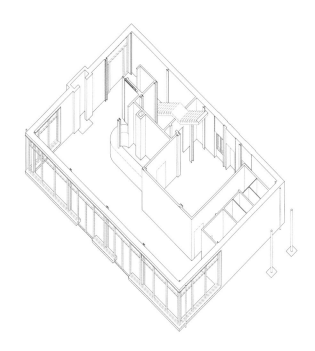

Axiometric of entrance level

Confer & Karnac, Spitalfields, London

Situated within the hinterland between Spitalfields and the City, Confer & Karnac is a cultural hub that fuses a range of different functions and purposes within one cohesive space. This is, on the one hand, a welcoming bookshop specialising in psychoanalysis and psychotherapy, along with related themes. At the same time, this is a base for a publishing house with two imprints of its own, dedicated to similar subject matter, as well as holding a dedicated events room and recording studio. Beyond this, Confer & Karnac also serves as an exhibition space, which has hosted work by a wide range of contemporary artists. Given this rich and unusual remit, a fully bespoke approach was required for the design.

'The clients were drawn to the location, on Strype Street, because of the artistic heritage of the area,' says Dyson. 'And they could see that we are connected both historically and artistically with the neighbourhood. The building that they found dates from the 1930s and is the shell of a former sequin factory, making sequins for haberdashery and the local garment industry, and it has these long, rectangular Crittall windows. So we drew on this, in part, for our palette of materials and the design scheme, particularly the glazing, the expressed columns and the use of plywood, which has this semi-industrial quality but is also a very warm material.'

The building itself had largely been converted to residential use during the 1990s, leaving a commercial space on the ground floor. Most recently, this unit had served as a bicycle retail store and workshop, and was spacious enough to accommodate the various needs of Confer & Karnac, while also benefitting from dual frontage on to both Strype Street and neighbouring Bell Lane. Flexibility was woven into the design and layout at every stage.

Left: Bar Social when open for book launches and events.

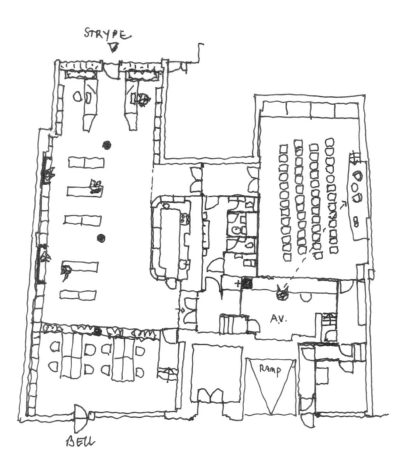

'The bookshop itself is a big space, with light from two sides, so wonderfully daylit,' says Dyson. 'On certain occasions, they have book launches and openings within the bookshop, so many of the plywood bookcases are mounted on castors so they can easily be moved out of the way when more space is needed. There's also a hidden bar and kitchenette at the centre of the plan, concealed within a display unit, which can also be brought into use for special events.'

Such thoughtfully tailored elements had to be balanced with the need for hanging space for artworks. These banks of open wall space are painted, like the circular pillars, in a vivid blue that is used throughout to enhance the sense of unity while contrasting gently with the plywood bookshelves and joinery.

'The blues and the pale green for the floors give the space this very calm feeling,' says Dyson. 'It's almost like an Yves Klein blue but we also discovered that blue is the company's corporate colour so we took inspiration from that as well. And then the ability to hang and display art is really the golden thread that helps to tie everything together.'

Above: Conceptual layout.
Right above: Rendering of interior.
Right below: Conference mode seating.

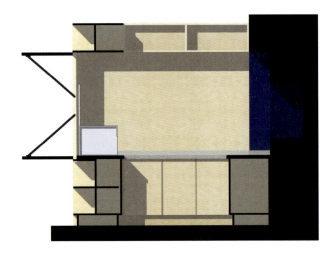
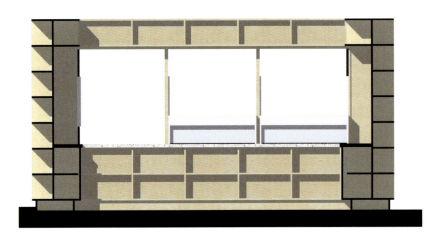
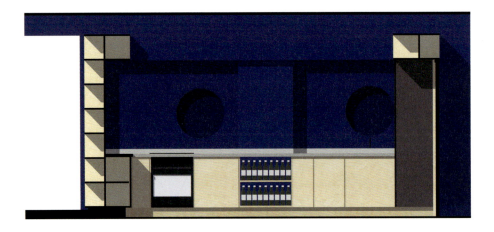

Above: Bar Social, blue and plywood.
Right: Recessed seating.

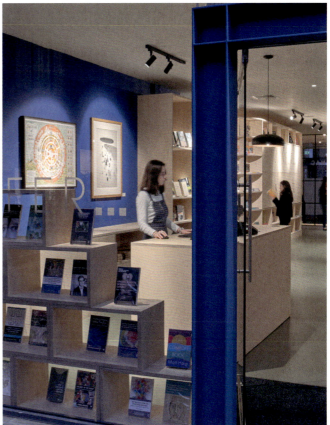

As well as providing niches and framed alcoves for displaying work by visiting artists, Dyson collaborated with artist Adam Dant, who was commissioned to design a bespoke artwork for the area behind the reception and sales desk. 'Adam made this radial psycho-geographic map for us to locate the shop but also worked on bookmarks and other things related to branding,' says Dyson. 'All of the furniture, including the counter and storage units, was designed by us and that also helps to tie the space together.'

Beyond the public realm of the bookshop, there are administration and service spaces. The other key element of the brief was the dedicated conference room for talks and live events. The provision of an adjoining studio and audio-visual suite means that Confer & Karnac can record these events for access on demand, while developing a growing archive of material focused on psychotherapy and mental health.

There is a great deal of ingenuity and technology threaded throughout the Confer & Karnac project. But, at the same time, the use of colour, natural materials and textures helps to create a soothing and engaging environment. More than this, the gallery element of the project adds another valuable layer of interest within a neighbourhood where art remains an essential ingredient.

Left: Bar Social open and closed.
Above: Curved bookshelving.
Above right: Entrance reception.

CULTURE & COMMUNITY: CONFER & KARNAC

Afterword
CHRIS DYSON

For us, design is an explicit and reiterative process beginning with research and analysis, which leads into conceptual exploration and development. We like to think of ourselves as architects who have sufficient means to make any commission a priority and I am fortunate to have a young and galvanized team. The office itself is both resolutely low and high-tech, while the hand is ever present, be it a sketch or a model.

Good design is drawn and the effectiveness of drawing is based on the precision with which it succeeds in identifying and prefiguring the ways in which the building will be made. A good architect says: 'I will draw this to convey this'. Everything has its purpose beyond mere style and perhaps the most intense example is the detail drawing, while the most lucid is the conceptual drawing, with each of these often born of different mind sets. However, one is no good at all without the other, or without a vision of the whole and its full potential. An excellent draughtsman by computer, or by hand, is to be much admired and neither is superior to the other, so long as the design has purpose in mind. Renderings, sketches and physical models are also essential to our craft.

Presently, we build at a variety of scales. Most of us have experienced design studios with larger public projects and within this book you will certainly find a few examples. I believe the same intensity applies to the larger projects as to the smaller commissions, often revisiting and checking along the critical process of design, through to definition in the working drawings and tenders to build.

Left: Rear view of Albion Drive extension.

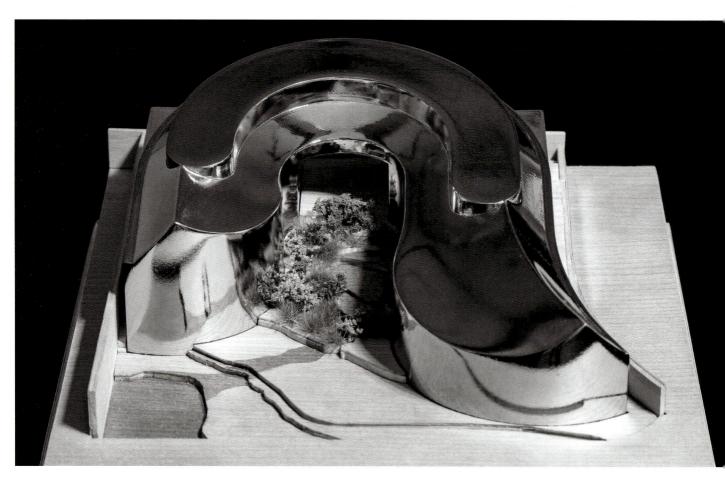

As a small team practice, each architect 'carries' these responsibilities with great care and effectiveness, often working with a variety of craftsmen and subcontractors on the smaller commissions and liaising with the main contractor on the larger projects. The act of drawing requires a good mind and must always say something, such as 'here is the brick arch and this is how it sits in relation to the window frame and sill', par example. For this we gain both the respect of our clients, as well as the contractor, and in this act we become masters of our craft, which is making well-built and useful buildings to last for as long as the materials will allow.

CDA has grown a little more since our last book, *Practice & Projects* published by Artifice books. We have made forays into larger scale projects and competitions, with some of these illustrated within this book. We remain committed to the well-chosen and occasional design competition, often spinning plates between planning submissions and detail design and

Left above: Paxton Lodge 'Cascades', a two-house proposal.
Above: Cultural building view from Brick Lane.

execution on site. We seek to vitalise contemporary architecture with a rich, inclusive architectural language, which fuses the modern movement's ideals of functionality, clarity, integrity and economy with the traditional architectural qualities of form, space and thereby conveys a sense of historical continuity. We are also striving for a synthesis between the monumental tradition of public building with the more informal and accessible image of culture today. Above all, we hope to maintain the connection between suitability for purpose and beauty.

Behind every successful building is an engaged and proactive Client, who makes a unique contribution to the development of the brief and evolution of the design. For us, such engagement across all stages of the design and construction process is crucial. Ideally, we become involved in a project when the initial activity and spatial brief of requirements and site have been established and we can then contribute with the Client, as well as specialist consultants, to the development of its full potential.

In short, we welcome Client input into an open and all-encompassing design process. We do not have a 'house style' and do not impose preconceived ideas upon unique situations. Each of our designs evolves from the particular circumstances and opportunities of each brief as well as the physical context. The size of our practice and workload is optimised to enable us to provide a truly personal service to our Clients from inception, through design, to the completion and occupation of a building. This means attendance by the principal and associates at all Client meetings throughout the project.

We are creative, nimble and devoted to our projects. All of our staff are qualified architects and we do not have other in-house disciplines, as we prefer to assemble an appropriate team of consultants for each individual project, combining our design abilities with the best available technical expertise. In a practice of this size, from table top sketch, model and computer drawings to physical reality, a small army of people are involved. Some are present from the beginning to the end, while others contribute for just a short time or a specific purpose. But everyone involved counts and everyone makes a difference. My gratitude goes out to those listed at the back of this volume, along with many others too numerous to mention. Speaking for all of us at Chris Dyson Architects, we very much hope that you will enjoy the book and our work.

CD June 2023

Right: House and terraces in Moltedo, near Imperia, Liguria, Italy.

Chronology

2008
Princelet Street,
Spitalfields, London

2009
Chanarin Residence & Studio,
Spitalfields, London

2010
Faulkner Residence,
Spitalfields, London

2013
Wapping Pierhead,
Wapping, London

2015
The Cooperage,
Clerkenwell, London

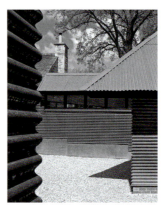

2015
Gasworks,
Gloucestershire

2015
Timothy Everest Store,
Shoreditch, London

2017
Eleven Spitalfields Gallery,
Spitalfields, London

2017
The Queen's Head,
Spitalfields, London

2018
The Sekforde,
Clerkenwell, London

2019
Crystal Palace Park Café,
Bromley, London

2020
Albion Works,
Hackney, London

2020
Confer & Karnac,
Spitalfields, London

2020
Hampton Lodge,
Hurstpierpoint, West Sussex

2015–22
Architect's Home & Studio,
Preston St Mary, Suffolk

2015–22
Maison Colbert,
London

CHRONOLOGY

Acknowledgements

This book came into being after being approached by Val Rose and Dominic Bradbury and I am much indebted to Lund Humphries and all those who have contributed to the publication and, in particular, to Associate Diana Raican for assembling the material, as well as Sarah Thorowgood, Tom Green and Val Rose and the rest of the team at Lund Humphries. My thanks for their generous words also go to: Richard Griffiths, Owen Hopkins, Jock McFadyen, Peter Murray, Humphrey Ocean and Charles Saumarez Smith.

Also with grateful thanks to the following staff whose contributions have been many and varied: Olusola Adebakin, Michael Archer, Tom Atkinson, Alexandra Baidac, Julia Bednarek, Uta Boecker, John Bowmer, Yasmin Braa, Paul Broadbent, Victoria Bromm, Vanessa Campanelli, Clara Carnot, Sang Min Cha, Hing Chan, Alice Cheung, James Cheung, Stephanie Cheung, Darren Clements, Mark Coles, Corinne Davidson, Karen Dawson, Ellisse Dixon, Margaret Dunn, Oliver Dunn, Oliver Dyson, Muireann Egan, Aaron English, Marina Furlanetto, Alice Grant, Estelle Hobeika, Angelito Huang, Matt Hurley, Freddie Hutchinson, Austin Joseph, Jessica Karlsson, Josephine Kawiche, Yashin Kemal, Jorge Khawam, Anna Kubelik, Petra Topsy Kustrin, Andrew Lang, Anita Lawlor, Jacqueline Leckenby, Louis Liu, Maria-Louise Long, Lila Macfarlane, Julie Maclean, Georgie Mann, Frank Maurer, Fiona McGarvey, Rosie McLaren, Katrin Meincke, Aranzazu Melon, Jessica Morley, Alice Moxley, Nic Murraine, Jason Ng, Andrew O'Driscoll, Louis O'Hanlon, Tom Pande, Alice Parker, Tomas Payani Gunnarsson, Berith Pederson, Viola Pelu, Michael Perry, Samuel Pew Latter, Oscar Plastow, Alina Popa, Marlene Probst, Gideon Purser, Ash Rahman, Diana Raican, Liam Rendall, Michael Roberts, Jack Rowlinson, Louis Russell, Delia Scarpellino, Karsten Schulz, Bahar Seyed Tabatabaei, Nilesh Shah, Koryn Steinbok, Malissa Talyor, Neil Taylor, Alice Theodorou, Sarah Thomas, Elodie Vidal, Harry Whittaker, Alannah Wilson, Mathew Witts, Victoria Yakovets, Yuma Yamamoto, Drew Yates.

Finally, I would like to acknowledge the inspiration and patience of my family: Sarah a teacher, Oliver an architect, Isabella an artist.